Charted Designs for the Kitchen

From the Archives of the
Lindberg Press

DOVER PUBLICATIONS, INC., NEW YORK

Copyright © 1987 by Dover Publications, Inc.
All rights reserved under Pan American and International Copyright Conventions.

Published in Canada by General Publishing Company, Ltd.,
30 Lesmill Road, Don Mills, Toronto, Ontario.
Published in the United Kingdom by Constable and Company, Ltd.,
10 Orange Street, London WC2H 7EG.

Charted Designs for the Kitchen is a new work, first published
by Dover Publications, Inc., in 1987.

Manufactured in the United States of America
Dover Publications, Inc.
31 East 2nd Street
Mineola, N.Y. 11501

Library of Congress Cataloging-in-Publication Data

Charted designs for the kitchen.

1. Needlework—Patterns. I. Lindberg Press.
TT753.C47 1987   746.9   87-13623
ISBN 0-486-25496-8 (pbk.)

Introduction

The kitchen is one of the most important rooms in the modern home. Not only are meals prepared and often eaten there, but the kitchen also serves as an unofficial den, office, playroom and family message center. We eat, work, play and visit all in the kitchen.

Because the kitchen is so important, decorating—and redecorating—it has become a national pastime. One of the simplest ways to brighten up your kitchen is to add hand-embroidered accessories such as placemats, potholders, doilies and shelf edgings. The photographs on the covers of this book illustrate just a few of the possibilities.

The patterns offered here, created by some of Denmark's finest designers, include a wide range of designs from naturalistic peaches and pears to stylized rows of mushrooms or apples. No matter what your style of decorating, you are sure to find something here that will make the perfect accent.

Most of these designs were originally created for counted cross-stitch, but they are easily translated into other needlework techniques. Keep in mind that the finished piece will not be the same size as the charted design unless you are working on fabric or canvas with the same number of threads per inch as the chart has squares per inch. With knitting and crocheting, the size will vary according to the number of stitches per inch.

COUNTED CROSS-STITCH

MATERIALS

1. **Needles.** A small blunt tapestry needle, No. 24 or No. 26.
2. **Fabric.** Evenweave linen, cotton, wool or synthetic fabrics all work well. The most popular fabrics are aida cloth, linen and hardanger cloth. Cotton aida is most commonly available in 18 threads-per-inch, 14 threads-per-inch and 11 threads-per-inch (14-count is the most popular size). Evenweave linen comes in a variety of threads-per-inch. To work cross-stitch on linen involves a slightly different technique (see page 5). Thirty thread-per-inch linen will result in a stitch about the same size as 14-count aida. Hardanger cloth has 22 threads to the inch and is available in cotton or linen. The amount of fabric needed depends on the size of the cross-stitch design. To determine yardage, divide the number of stitches in the design by the thread-count of the fabric. For example: If a design 112 squares wide by 140 squares deep is worked on a 14-count fabric, divide 112 by 14 (= 8), and 140 by 14 (= 10). The design will measure 8″ × 10″. The same design worked on 22-count fabric measures about 5″ × 6½″.

3. **Threads and Yarns.** Six-strand embroidery floss, crewel wool, Danish Flower Thread, pearl cotton or metallic threads all work well for cross-stitch. DMC Embroidery Floss has been used to color-code the patterns in this volume; a conversion chart for Royal Mouliné Six-Strand Embroidery Floss from Coats & Clark, and Anchor Embroidery Floss from Susan Bates appears on page 48. Crewel wool works well on evenweave wool fabric. Danish Flower Thread is a thicker thread with a matte finish, one strand equaling two of embroidery floss.

4. **Embroidery Hoop.** A wooden or plastic 4″, 5″ or 6″ round or oval hoop with a screw-type tension adjuster works best for cross-stitch.

5. **Scissors.** A pair of sharp embroidery scissors is essential to all embroidery.

PREPARING TO WORK

To prevent raveling, either whip stitch or machine-stitch the outer edges of the fabric.

Locate the exact center of the chart (many of the charts in this book have an arrow at the top and side; follow these arrows to their intersection to locate the chart center). Establish the center of the fabric by folding it in half first vertically, then horizontally. The center stitch of the chart falls where the creases of the fabric meet. Mark the fabric center with a basting thread.

It is best to begin cross-stitch at the top of the design. To establish the top, count the squares up from the center of the chart, and the corresponding number of holes up from the center of the fabric.

Place the fabric tautly in the embroidery hoop, for tension makes it easier to push the needle through the holes without piercing the fibers. While working continue to retighten the fabric as necessary.

When working with multiple strands (such as embroidery floss) always separate (strand) the thread before beginning to stitch. This one small step allows for better coverage of the fabric. When you need more than one thread in the needle, use separate strands and do not double the thread. (For example: If you need four strands, use four separated strands.) Thread has a nap (just as fabrics do) and can be felt to be smoother in one direction than the other. Always work with the nap (the smooth side) pointing down.

For 14-count aida and 30-count linen, work with two strands of six-strand floss. For more texture, use more thread; for a flatter look, use less thread.

EMBROIDERY

To begin, fasten the thread with a waste knot and hold a short length of thread on the underside of the work, anchoring it with the first few stitches (*Diagram 1*). When the thread end is securely in place, clip the knot.

DIAGRAM 1
Reverse side of work

To stitch, push the needle up through a hole in the fabric, cross the thread intersection (or square) on a left-to-right diagonal (*Diagram 2*). Half the stitch is now completed.

DIAGRAM 2

Next, cross back, right to left, forming an X (*Diagram 3*).

DIAGRAM 3

DIAGRAM 4

Work all the same color stitches on one row, then cross back, completing the X's (*Diagram 4*).

Some needleworkers prefer to cross each stitch as they come to it. This method also works, but be sure all of the top stitches are slanted in the same direction. Isolated stitches must be crossed as they are worked. Vertical stitches are crossed as shown in *Diagram 5*.

DIAGRAM 5

At the top, work horizontal rows of a single color, left to right. This method allows you to go from an unoccupied space to an occupied space (working from an empty hole to a filled one), making ruffling of the floss less likely. Holes are used more than once, and all stitches "hold hands" unless a space is indicated on the chart. Hold the work upright throughout (do not turn as with many needlepoint stitches).

When carrying the thread from one area to another, run the needle under a few stitches on the wrong side. Do not carry thread across an open expanse of fabric as it will be visible from the front when the project is completed.

To end a color, weave in and out of the underside of the stitches, making a scallop stitch or two for extra security (*Diagram 6*). When possible, end in the same direction in which you were working, jumping up a row if necessary (*Diagram 7*). This prevents holes caused by stitches being pulled in two directions. Trim the thread ends closely and do not leave any tails or knots as they will show through the fabric when the work is completed.

A number of other counted-thread stitches can be used in cross-stitch. Backstitch (*Diagram 8*) is used for outlines, face details and the like. It is worked from hole to hole, and may be stitched as a vertical, horizontal or diagonal line.

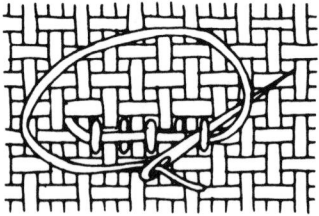

DIAGRAM 6
Reverse side of work

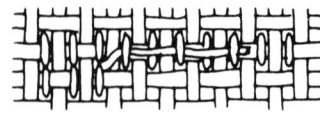

DIAGRAM 7
Reverse side of work

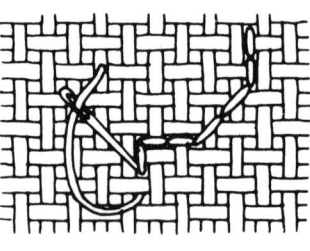

DIAGRAM 8

Straight stitch is worked from side to side over several threads (*Diagram 9*) and affords solid coverage.

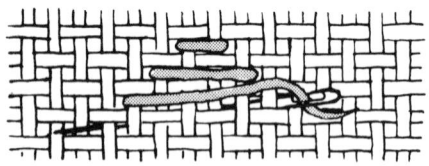

DIAGRAM 9

Lazy daisy stitch and chain stitch (*Diagram 10*) are handy for special effects. Both are worked in the same manner as on regular embroidery.

Lazy Daisy Stitch

Chain Stitch

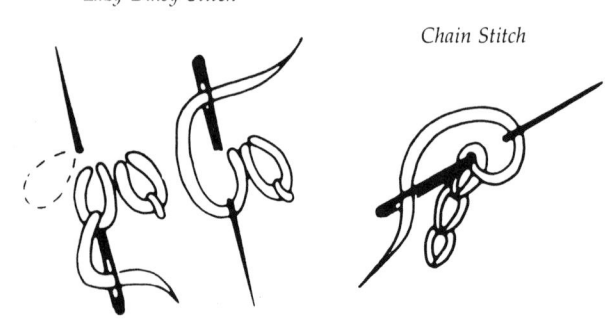

DIAGRAM 10

4

Embroidery on Linen. Working on linen requires a slightly different technique. While evenweave linen is remarkably regular, there are always a few thick or thin threads. To keep the stitches even, cross-stitch is worked over two threads in each direction (*Diagram 11*).

DIAGRAM 11

As you are working over more threads, linen affords a greater variation in stitches. A half-stitch can slant in either direction and is uncrossed. A three-quarters stitch is shown in *Diagram 12*.

DIAGRAM 12

Diagram 13 shows the backstitch worked on linen.

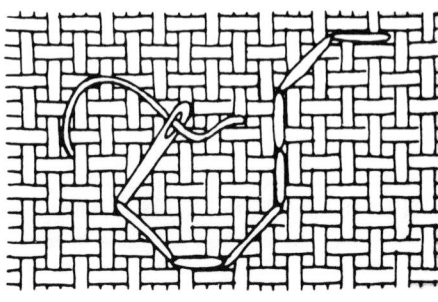

DIAGRAM 13

Embroidery on Gingham. Gingham and other checked fabrics can be used for cross-stitch. Using the fabric as a guide, work the stitches from corner to corner of each check.

Embroidery on Uneven-Weave Fabrics. If you wish to work cross-stitch on an uneven-weave fabric, baste a lightweight Penelope needlepoint canvas to the material. The design can then be stitched by working the cross-stitch over the double mesh of the canvas. When working in this manner, take care not to catch the threads of the canvas in the embroidery. After the cross-stitch is completed, remove the basting threads. With tweezers remove first the vertical threads, one strand at a time, of the needlepoint canvas, then the horizontal threads.

NEEDLEPOINT

One of the most common methods for working needlepoint is from a charted design. By simply viewing each square of a chart as a stitch on the canvas, the patterns quickly and easily translate from one technique to another.

MATERIALS

1. **Needles.** A blunt tapestry needle with a rounded tip and an elongated eye. The needle must clear the hole of the canvas without spreading the threads. For No. 10 canvas, a No. 18 needle works best.

2. **Canvas.** There are two distinct types of needlepoint canvas: single-mesh (mono canvas) and double-mesh (Penelope canvas). Single-mesh canvas, the more common of the two, is easier on the eyes as the spaces are slightly larger. Double-mesh canvas has two horizontal and two vertical threads forming each mesh. The latter is a very stable canvas on which the threads stay securely in place as the work progresses. Canvas is available in many sizes, from 5 mesh-per-inch to 18 mesh-per-inch, and even smaller. The number of mesh-per-inch will, of course, determine the dimensions of the finished needlepoint project. A 60 square × 120 square chart will measure 12″ × 24″ on 5 mesh-to-the-inch canvas, 5″ × 10″ on 12 mesh-to-the-inch canvas. The most common canvas size is 10 to the inch.

3. **Yarns.** Persian, crewel and tapestry yarns all work well on needlepoint canvas.

PREPARING TO WORK

Allow 1″ to 1½″ blank canvas all around. Bind the raw edges of the canvas with masking tape or machine-stitched double-fold bias tape.

There are few hard-and-fast rules on where to begin the design. It is best to complete the main motif, then fill the background as the last step.

For any guidelines you wish to draw on the canvas, take care that your marking medium is waterproof. Nonsoluble inks, acrylic paints thinned with water so as not to clog the mesh, and waterproof felt-tip pens all work well. If unsure, experiment on a scrap of canvas.

When working with multiple strands (such as Persian yarn) always separate (strand) the yarn before beginning to stitch. This one small step allows for better coverage of the canvas. When you need more than one piece of yarn in the needle, use separate strands and do not double the yarn. For example: If you need two strands of 3-ply Persian yarn, use two separated strands. Yarn has a nap (just as fabrics do) and can be felt to be smoother in one direction than the other. Always work with the nap (the smooth side) pointing down.

For 5 mesh-to-the-inch canvas, use six strands of 3-ply yarn; for 10 mesh-to-the-inch canvas, use three strands of 3-ply yarn.

STITCHING

Cut yarn lengths 18″ long. Begin needlepoint by holding about 1″ of loose yarn on the wrong side of the work and working the first several stitches over the loose end to secure it. To end a piece of yarn, run it under several completed stitches on the wrong side of the work.

There are hundreds of needlepoint stitch variations, but tent stitch is universally considered to be *the* needlepoint stitch. The most familiar versions of tent stitch are half-cross stitch, continental stitch and basket-weave stitch.

Half-cross stitch (*Diagram 14*) is worked from left to right. The canvas is then turned around and the return row is again stitched from left to right. Holding the needle vertically, bring it to the front of the canvas through the hole that will

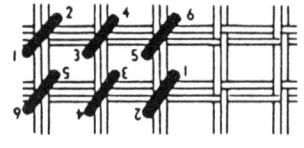

DIAGRAM 14

be the bottom of the first stitch. Keep the stitches loose for minimum distortion and good coverage. Half-cross stitch is best worked on a double-mesh canvas.

Continental stitch (*Diagram 15*) begins in the upper right-hand corner and is worked from right to left. The needle is slanted and always brought out a mesh ahead. The resulting stitch appears as a half-cross stitch on the front and as a slanting stitch on the back. When the row is complete, turn the canvas around to work the return row, continuing to stitch from right to left.

DIAGRAM 15

Basket-weave stitch (*Diagram 16*) begins in the upper right-hand corner with four continental stitches (two stitches worked horizontally across the top and two placed directly below the first stitch). Work diagonal rows, the first slanting up and across the canvas from right to left, and the next down and across from left to right. Moving down the canvas from left to right, the needle is in a vertical position; working in the opposite direction, the needle is horizontal. The rows interlock, creating a basket-weave pattern on the wrong side. If the stitch is not done properly, a faint ridge will show where the pattern was interrupted. On basket-weave stitch, always stop working in the middle of a row, rather than at the end, so that you will know in which direction you were working.

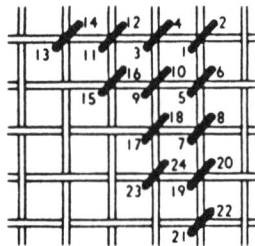

DIAGRAM 16

KNITTING

Charted designs can be worked into stockinette stitch as you are knitting, or they can be embroidered with duplicate stitch when the knitting is complete. For the former, wind the different colors of yarn on bobbins and work in the same manner as in Fair Isle knitting. A few quick Fair Isle tips: (1) Always bring up the new color yarn from under the dropped color to prevent holes. (2) Carry the color not in use loosely across the wrong side of the work, but not more than three or four stitches without twisting the yarns. If a color is not in use for more than seven or eight stitches, it is usually best to drop that color yarn and rejoin a new bobbin when the color is again needed.

CROCHET

There are a number of ways in which charts can be used for crochet. Among them are:

SINGLE CROCHET

Single crochet is often seen worked in multiple colors. When changing colors, always pick up the new color for the last yarn-over of the old color. The color not in use can be carried loosely across the back of the work for a few stitches, or you can work the single crochet over the unused color. The latter method makes for a neater appearance on the wrong side, but sometimes the old color peeks through the stitches. This method can also be applied to half-double crochet and double crochet, but keep in mind that the longer stitches will distort the design.

FILET CROCHET

This technique is nearly always worked from charts and uses only one color thread. The result is a solid-color piece with the design filled in and the background left as an open mesh. Care must be taken in selecting the design, as the longer stitch causes distortion.

AFGHAN CROCHET

The most common method here is cross-stitch worked over the afghan stitch. Complete the afghan crochet project. Then, following the chart for color placement, work cross-stitch over the squares of crochet.

OTHER CHARTED METHODS

Latch hook, Assisi embroidery, beading, cross-stitch on needlepoint canvas (a European favorite) and lace net embroidery are among the other needlework methods worked from charts.

Peach

	DMC #	
▼	469	Avocado Green
☑	470	Medium Light Avocado Green
☒	471	Light Avocado Green
⊞	472	Very Light Avocado Green
◿	3347	Medium Yellow Green
▲	783	Christmas Gold
⊡	725	Topaz
◪	817	Very Dark Coral
⊞	347	Dark Salmon
◎	3328	Medium Salmon
⊟	760	Salmon
◪	400	Dark Mahogany
◭	301	Medium Mahogany

Cherries

	DMC #	
⊙	349	Dark Coral
⊠	351	Coral
◺	352	Light Coral
⊡	353	Peach
◩	840	Medium Beige Brown
☑	842	Very Light Beige Brown
■	904	Very Dark Parrot Green
▼	905	Dark Parrot Green
◪	907	Light Parrot Green
—	907	Light Parrot Green backstitch

8

Pear

	DMC #	
◪	680	Dark Old Gold
⊙	729	Medium Old Gold
⊟	676	Light Old Gold
⊡	677	Very Light Old Gold
■	838	Very Dark Beige Brown
◪	840	Medium Beige Brown
⊻	842	Very Light Beige Brown
▼	904	Very Dark Parrot Green
⊠	905	Dark Parrot Green
◩	906	Medium Parrot Green
⊞	907	Light Parrot Green

Plums

	DMC #	
☒	824	Very Dark Blue
⊡	813	Light Blue
☑	841	Light Beige Brown
▼	905	Dark Parrot Green
◪	906	Medium Parrot Green
⊞	907	Light Parrot Green

Apple

	DMC #	
▼	367	Dark Pistachio Green
◹	320	Medium Pistachio Green
⊞	368	Light Pistachio Green
⊿	3347	Medium Yellow Green
◤	347	Dark Salmon
⊞	3328	Medium Salmon
⊘	760	Salmon
⊡	761	Light Salmon
■	839	Dark Beige Brown
⊻	840	Medium Beige Brown

Lemon

DMC #

☑	444	Dark Lemon Yellow
⊡	307	Lemon Yellow
⊡	445	Light Lemon Yellow
◪	739	Fawn Beige
▼	987	Medium Forest Green
☒	988	Forest Green
◹	989	Light Forest Green
⊞	368	Pale Pistachio Green
■	840	Medium Beige Brown

Red Currant

DMC #

⊙	350	Medium Coral
▼	700	Bright Christmas Green
⊠	702	Kelly Green
⊡	703	Chartreuse
◪	839	Dark Beige Brown
—	839	Dark Beige Brown back-stitch
⬦	841	Light Beige Brown

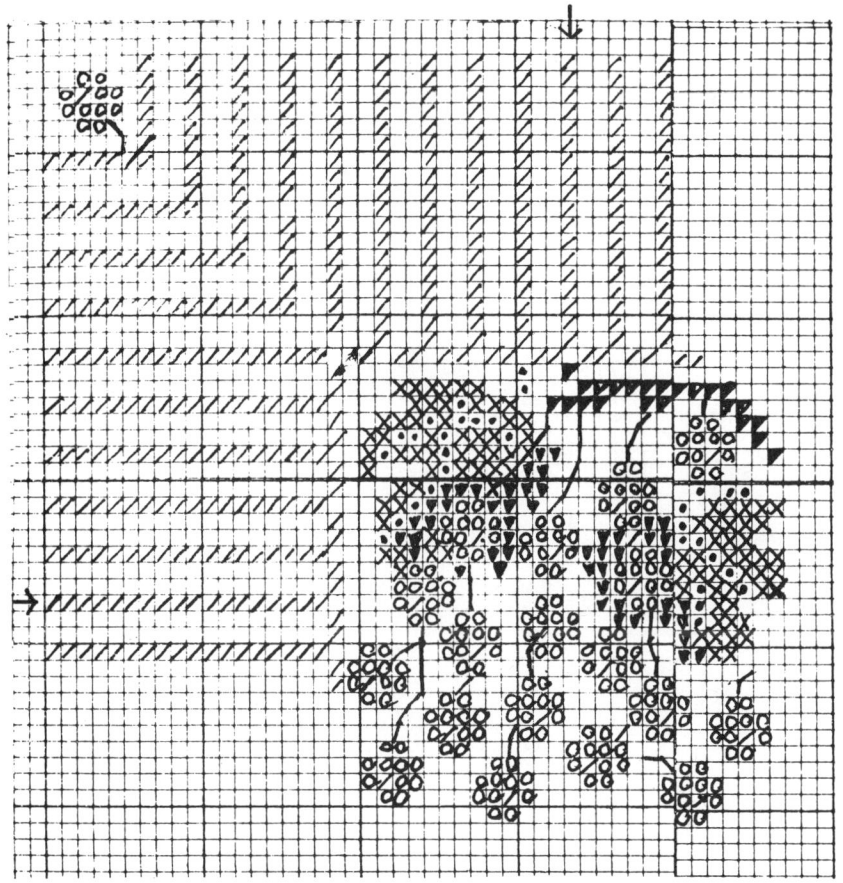

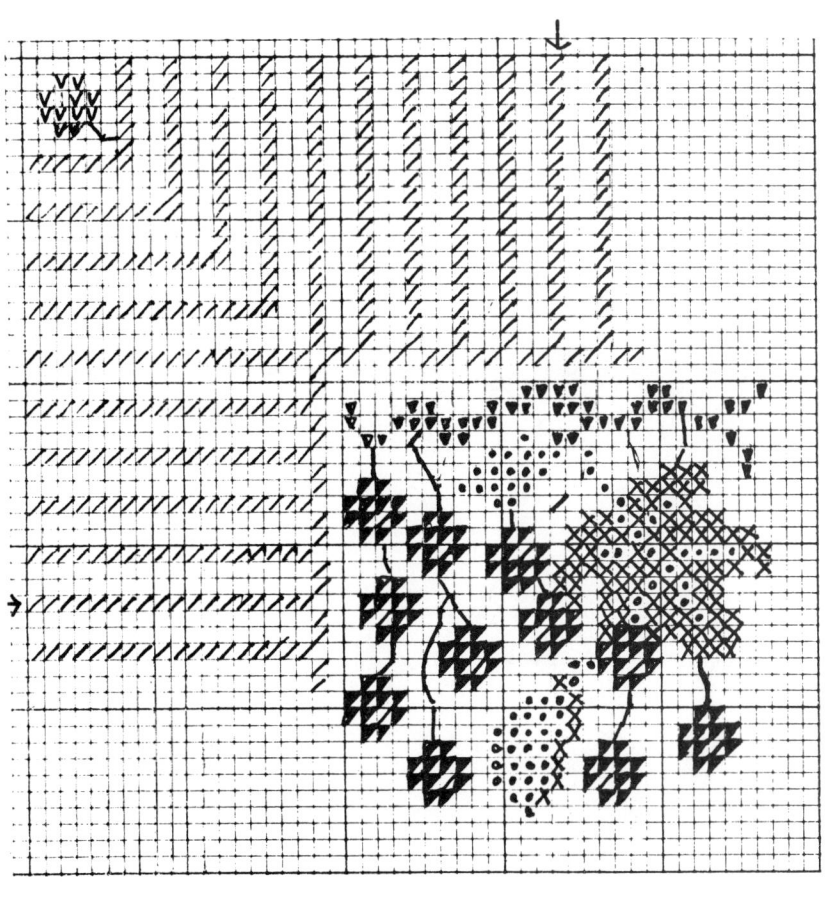

Black Currant

DMC #

◪	823	Dark Navy Blue
⊠	702	Kelly Green
⊡	703	Chartreuse
▼	839	Dark Beige Brown
⊞	841	Light Beige Brown
—	841	Light Beige Brown back-stitch

Coffee

DMC #					
◩	987	Medium Forest Green	⊟ {	369	Pale Pistachio Green
◪	988	Forest Green			White
⊞	989	Light Forest Green			Use 1 strand of each color
⊠	3347	Medium Yellow Green	•	310	Black backstitch
◉	3348	Light Yellow Green	—	727	Very Light Topaz backstitch
◪ {	3347	Medium Yellow Green	◪	814	Dark Garnet Red
	3348	Light Yellow Green	⊤	349	Dark Coral
		Use 1 strand of each color	◪	351	Coral
∿	368	Light Pistachio Green backstitch	⊡		White

Berries: Work a three-quarters cross-stitch in each corner—see detail. Add a Black backstitch at the center of each berry.

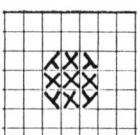

Berry Detail

14

Tea

▶	581	Moss Green		⊓	742	Light Tangerine
▼	3346	Hunter Green		◪	899	Medium Rose
⊠	3347	Medium Yellow Green		⑥	3326	Light Rose
⊙	3348	Light Yellow Green		⊔	776	Medium Pink
◪ {	3347	Medium Yellow Green				
	3348	Light Yellow Green				
		Use 1 strand of each color				

Cocoa

	DMC #							
▣	780	Very Dark Topaz	⊠	3347	Medium Yellow Green	⅃	839	Dark Beige Brown
⅂	782	Medium Topaz	⊡	3348	Light Yellow Green	⊠	841	Light Beige Brown
◥	783	Christmas Gold	◪ {	3347	Medium Yellow Green	—	841	Light Beige Brown backstitch
⊡	725	Topaz		3348	Light Yellow Green	◪	899	Medium Rose
⊡	726	Light Topaz			Use 1 strand of each color	⌇	899	Medium Rose backstitch
ⅴ	3346	Hunter Green	⊠	3053	Gray Green			

Vanilla

17

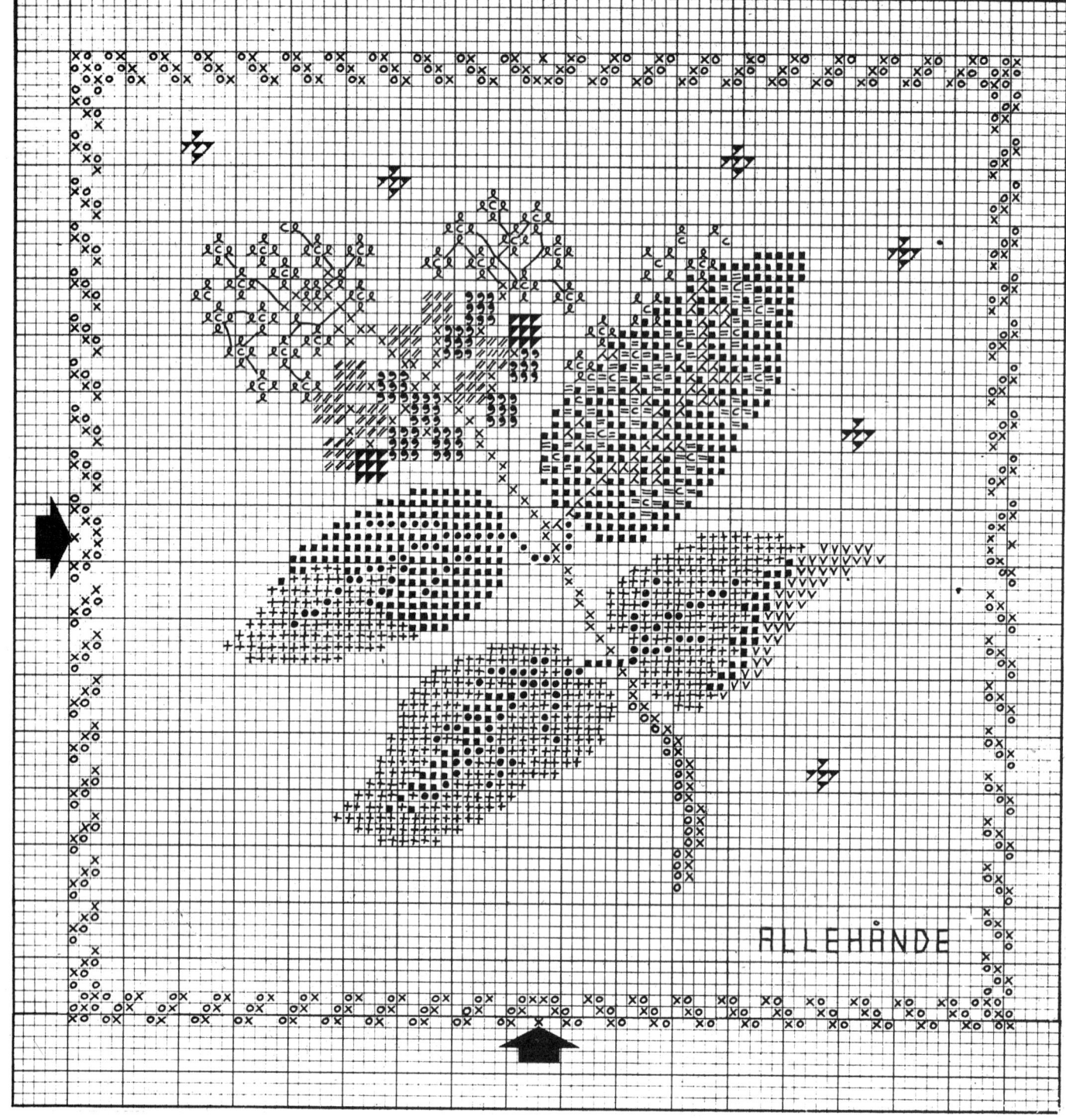

Allspice

DMC #

⊡	367	Dark Pistachio Green
■	988	Forest Green
⊞	989	Light Forest Green
☑	368	Light Pistachio Green
⊠ {	368	Light Pistachio Green / White Use 1 strand of each color
⊟ {	369	Pale Pistachio Green / White Use 1 strand of each color

⊠	471	Light Avocado Green
⊠	3347	Medium Yellow Green
—	3347	Medium Yellow Green backstitch
⊙	3348	Light Yellow Green
⊠ {	3347 / 3348	Medium Yellow Green / Light Yellow Green Use 1 strand of each color
◪	310	Black
◪	317	Pewter Gray

◪ {	310 / 317	Black / Pewter Gray Use 1 strand of each color
⊂	743	Dark Yellow

Berry Detail

Berries: Work a three-quarters cross-stitch in each corner—see detail.

18

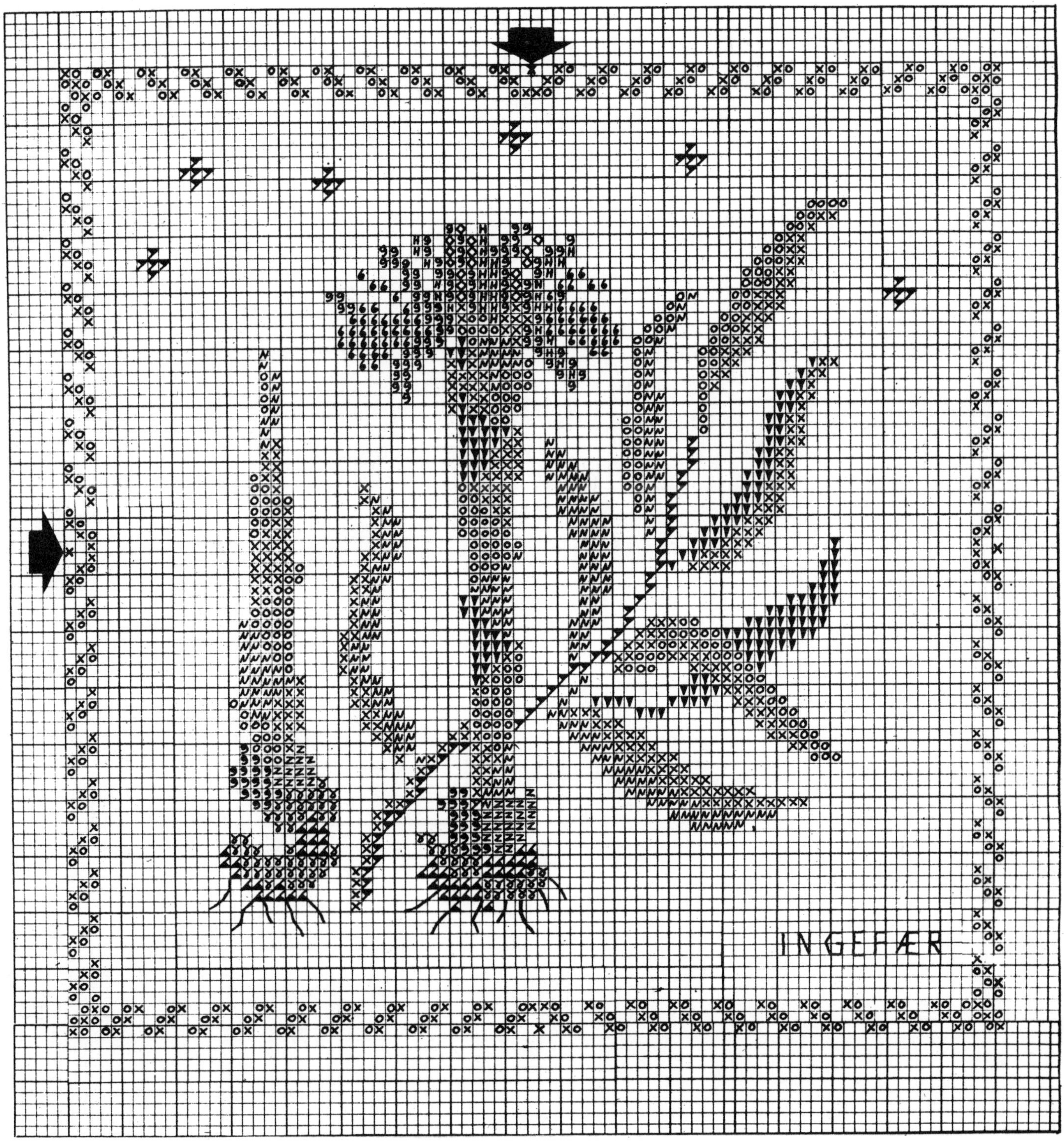

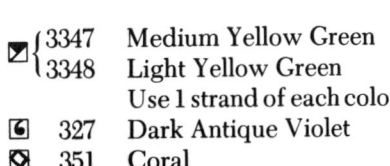

Ginger

Ⓝ	320	Medium Pistachio Green
Ⓢ	3012	Medium Khaki Green
Ⓩ	3013	Light Khaki Green
Ⓥ	3346	Hunter Green
Ⓧ	3347	Medium Yellow Green
Ⓞ	3348	Light Yellow Green

◪	{ 3347	Medium Yellow Green
	3348	Light Yellow Green
		Use 1 strand of each color
Ⓖ	327	Dark Antique Violet
Ⓞ	351	Coral
◪	611	Dark Drab Brown

—	611	Dark Drab Brown back-stitch
Ⓧ	612	Medium Drab Brown
Ⓗ	976	Medium Golden Brown
Ⓢ	977	Light Golden Brown

KRYDDERNELLIKE

Clove

20

Pepper

▨	3345	Dark Hunter Green
▼	3346	Hunter Green
⊠	3347	Medium Yellow Green
◙	3348	Light Yellow Green
◩ {	3347	Medium Yellow Green
	3348	Light Yellow Green
		Use 1 strand of each color

⊠	581	Moss Green
⊠	814	Dark Garnet Red
⊤	349	Dark Coral
⋰	351	Coral
│	310	Black backstitch

Berries: Work a three-quarters cross-

stitch in each corner—see detail.
Add a Black backstitch to each berry.

Berry Detail

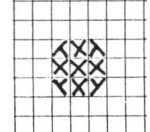

21

Capers

DMC #

▼	3346	Hunter Green	⊡ 347	Dark Salmon	
⊠	3347	Medium Yellow Green	— 3328	Medium Salmon backstitch—	
⊙	3348	Light Yellow Green		use 1 strand only	
◪ {	3347	Medium Yellow Green	···· 760	Salmon backstitch—use 1	
{	3348	Light Yellow Green		strand only	
		Use 1 strand of each color			

◪ { 356 Medium Terra-cotta
{ 3328 Medium Salmon
Use 1 strand of each color

⌄ 743 Dark Yellow backstitch

⊡ White

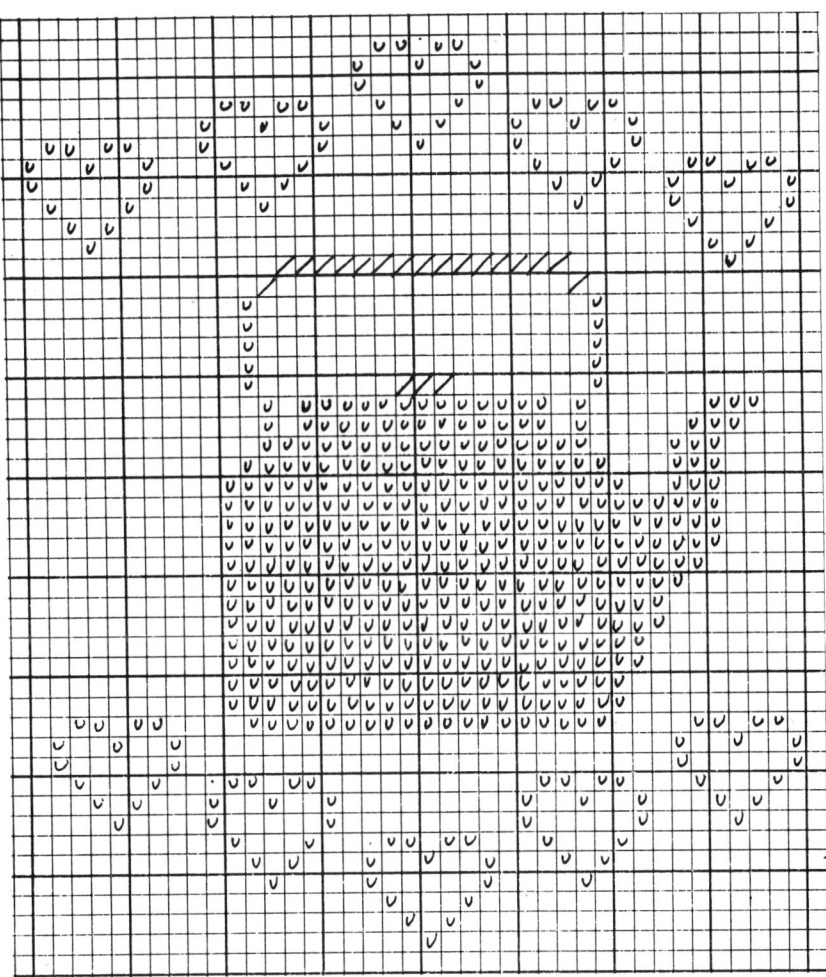

Teakettle Potholder

DMC #

⊘ 610   Very Dark Drab Brown
U 666   Bright Christmas Red

Kitchen Shelf Border

DMC #

⊡ 518   Light Wedgwood Blue

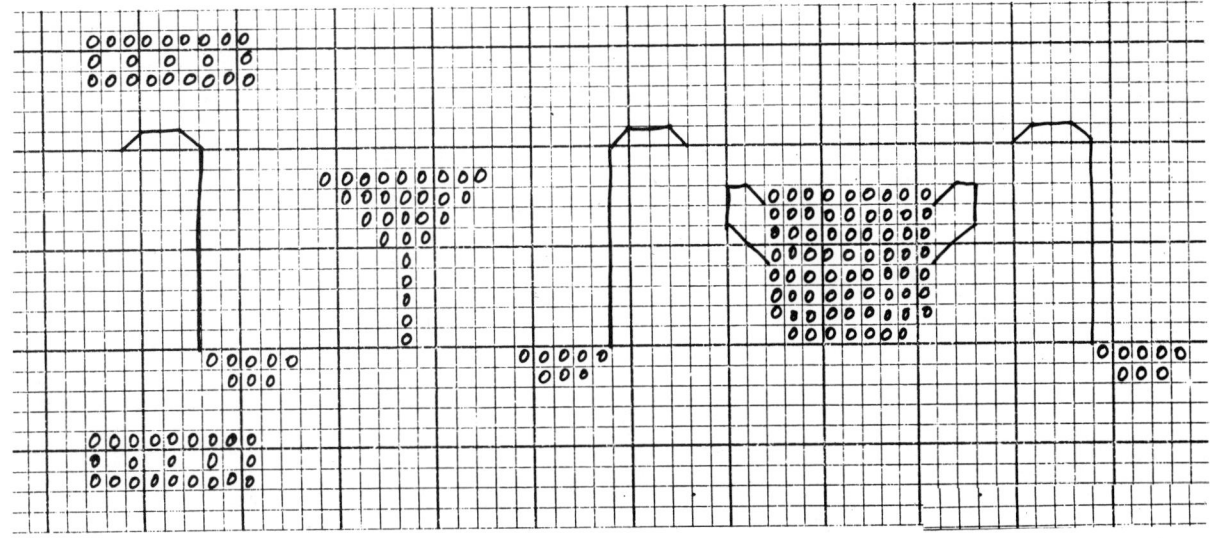

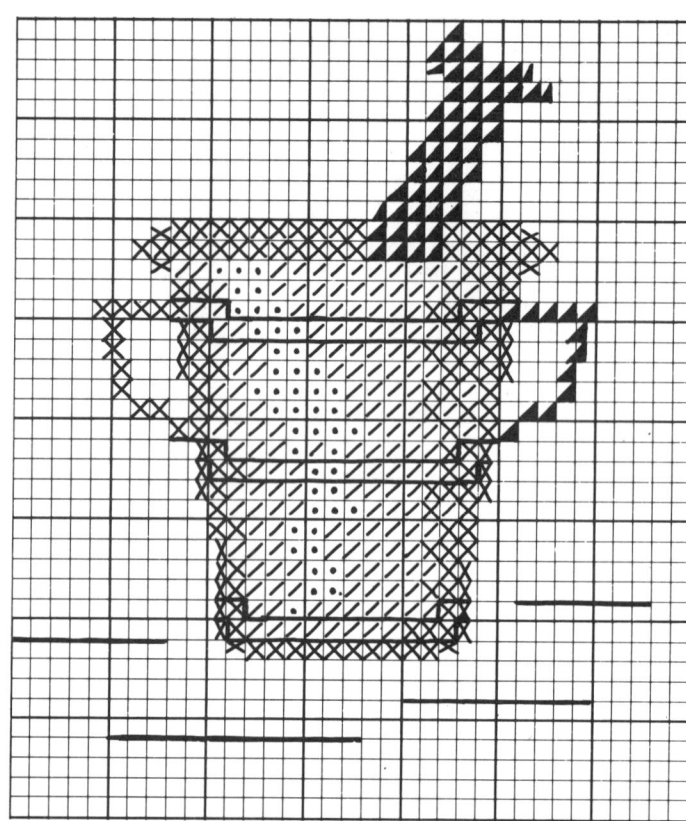

Mortar and Pestle

DMC #

◤	680	Dark Old Gold
☒	729	Medium Old Gold
◿	676	Light Old Gold
⊡	677	Very Light Old Gold
—	840	Medium Beige Brown backstitch

Coffeepot

DMC #

—	311	Medium Navy Blue back-stitch
▼	322	Dark Marine Blue
☒	334	Medium Marine Blue
⊡	3325	Baby Blue
∿	844	Ultra Dark Beaver Gray back-stitch

Soup Pot

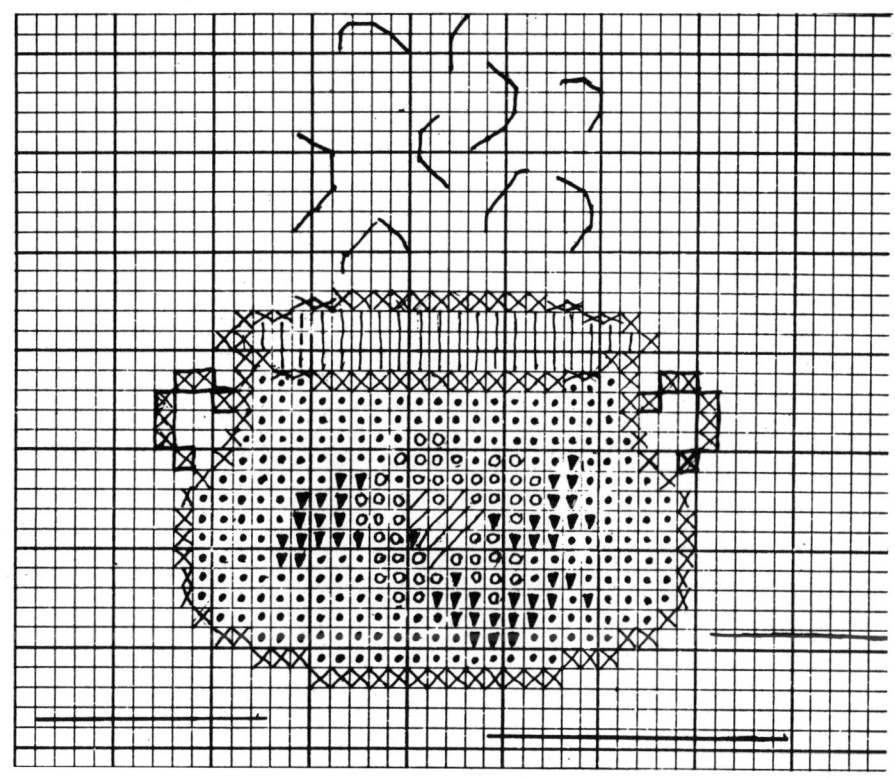

DMC #

⊠	334	Medium Marine Blue
⊡	3325	Baby Blue
—	3325	Baby Blue backstitch around handles
⊞	775	Light Baby Blue
—	775	Light Baby Blue backstitch over pot
▼	702	Kelly Green
⊘	729	Medium Old Gold
—	840	Medium Beige Brown backstitch under pot
⊙	891	Dark Carnation Red

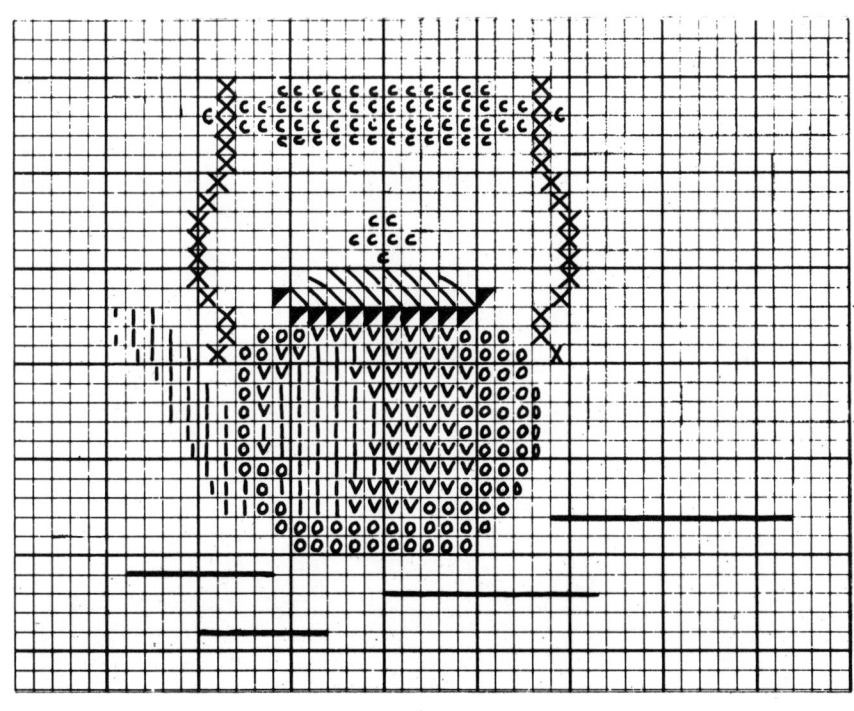

Teapot

DMC #

◩	919	Red Copper
⊙	921	Copper
☑	922	Light Copper
⊞	402	Very Light Mahogany
◪ {	922	Light Copper
	402	Very Light Mahogany Use 1 strand of each color
⊠	729	Medium Old Gold
ᴄ	840	Medium Beige Brown
—		Medium Beige Brown backstitch

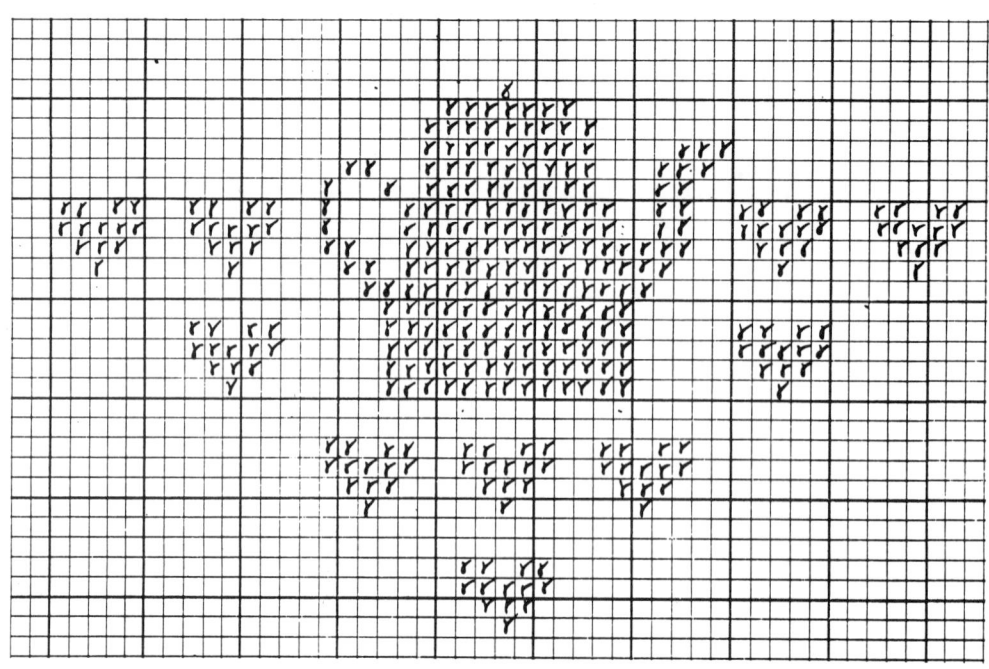

▲ I Love Coffee

DMC #

⊠   666   Bright Christmas Red

▼ Soup's On!

DMC #

☒   666   Bright Christmas Red
⊡   995   Dark Electric Blue

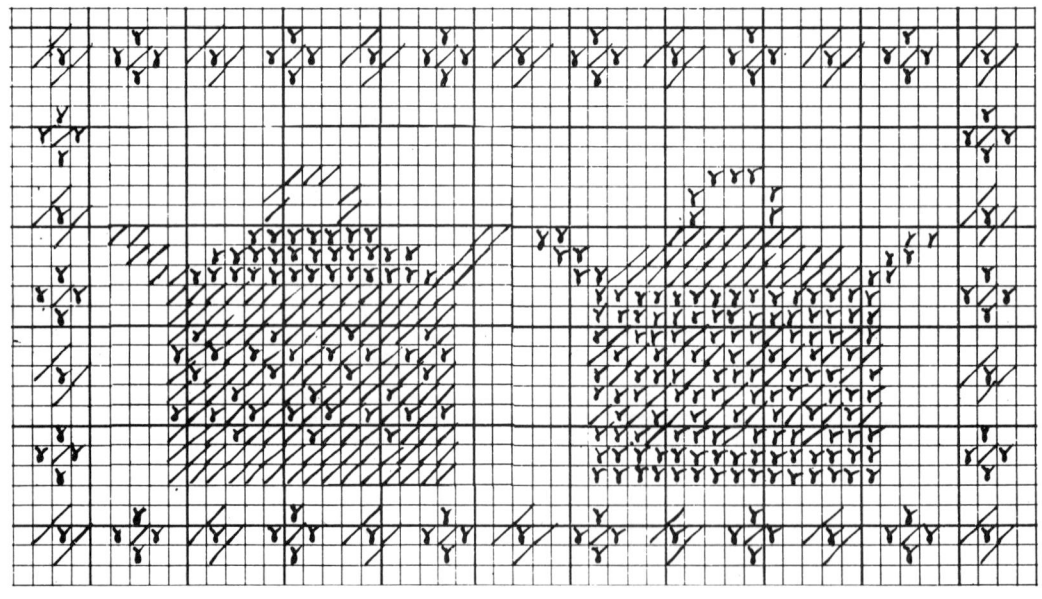

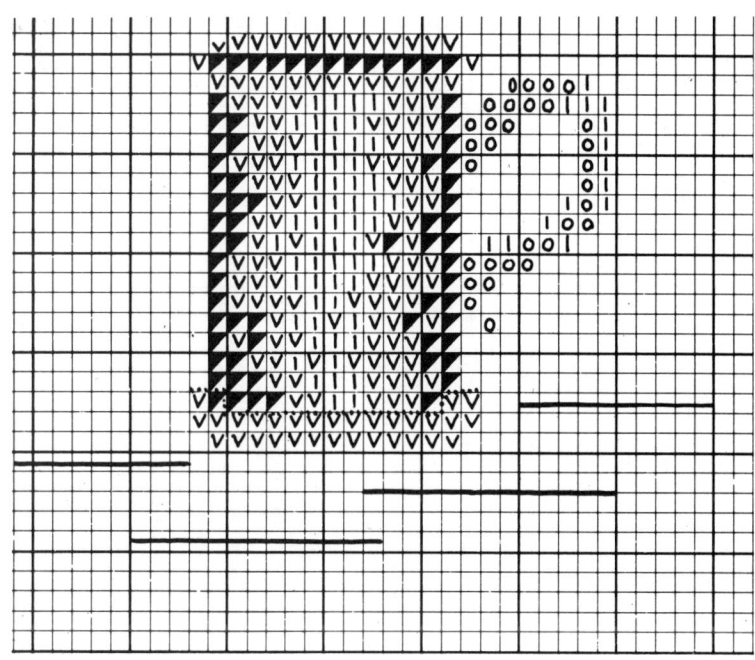

▲ Coffee Mug

DMC #

◪	919	Red Copper
••••	919	Red Copper backstitch
⊙	921	Copper
☑	922	Light Copper
⊡	402	Very Light Mahogany
—	840	Medium Beige Brown backstitch

▼ Coffee Break

DMC #

☑	666	Bright Christmas Red
⅄	995	Dark Electric Blue

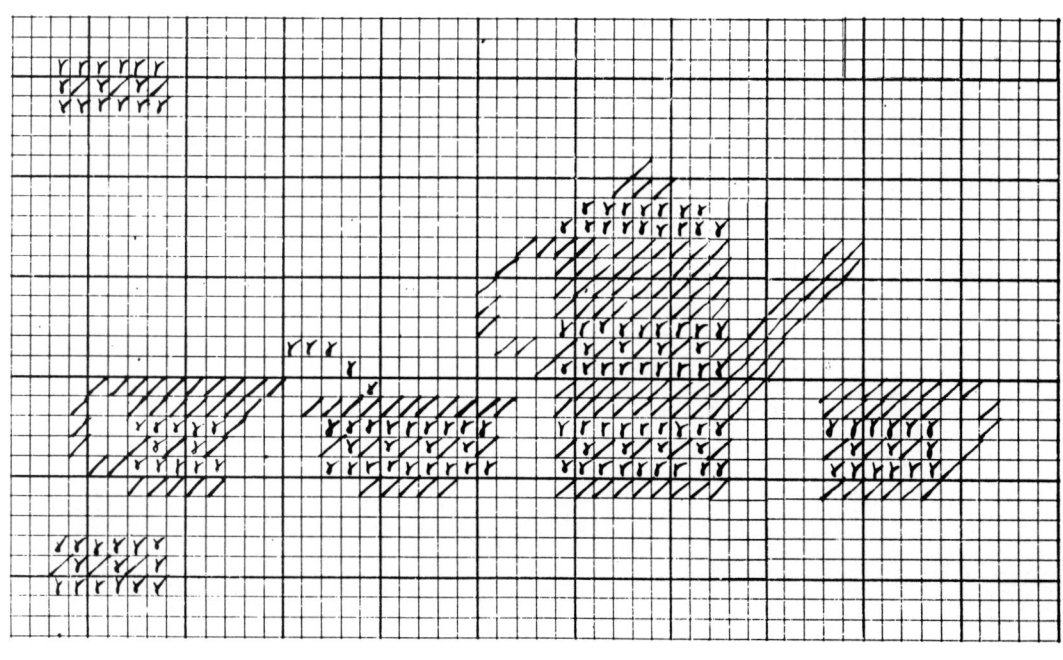

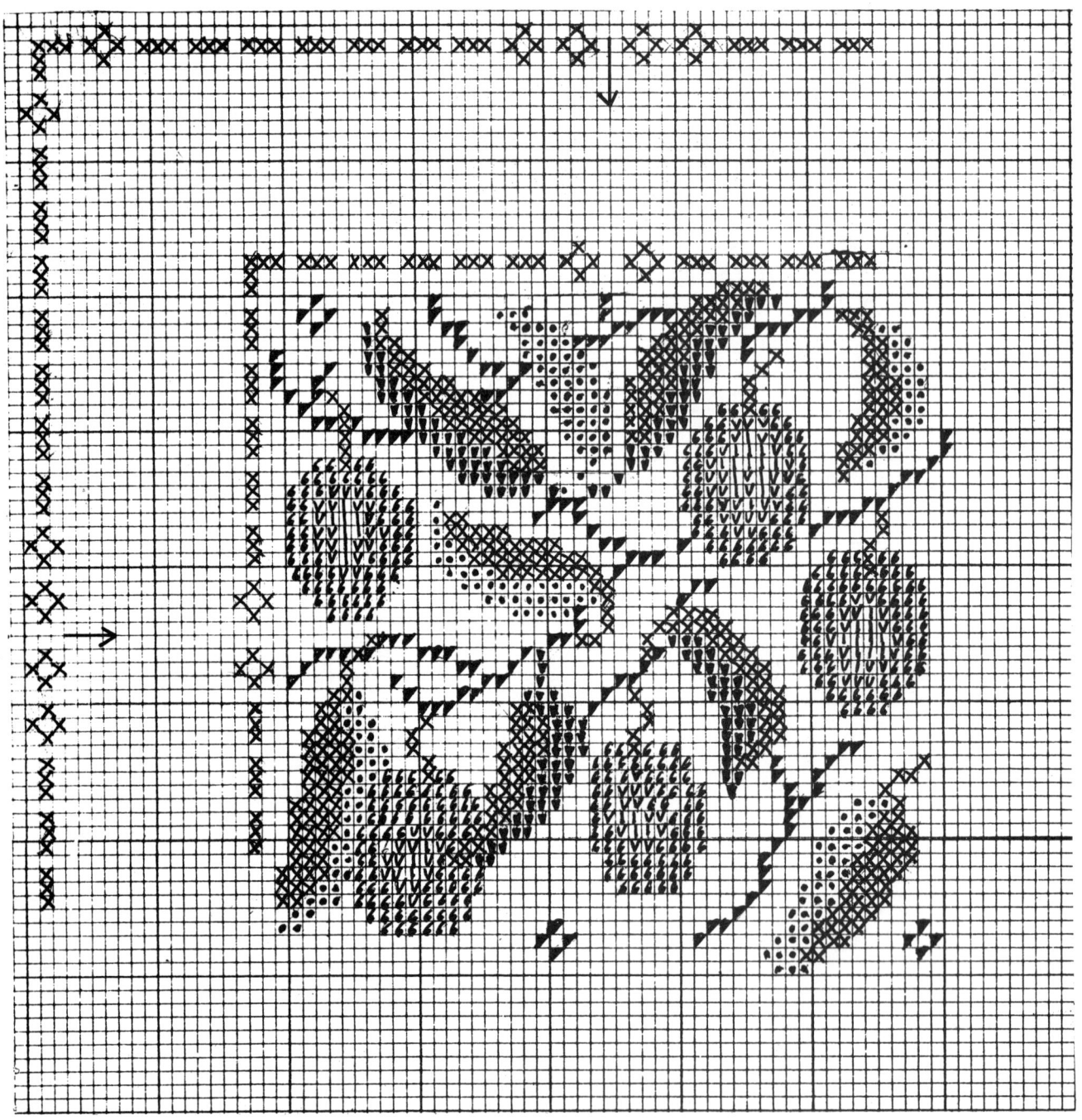

Plum Doily

DMC #

◖	312	Light Navy Blue
☑	334	Medium Marine Blue
①	3325	Baby Blue
▼	905	Dark Parrot Green
☒	906	Medium Parrot Green
·	907	Light Parrot Green
◤	840	Medium Beige Brown

Raspberry Doily

DMC #

▼	367	Dark Pistachio Green
☒	320	Medium Pistachio Green
⚠	368	Light Pistachio Green
⊞	369	Pale Pistachio Green
◪	347	Dark Salmon
⊙	3328	Medium Salmon
☑	760	Salmon
⊡	761	Light Salmon
⊻	407	Medium Cocoa Brown
—	407	Medium Cocoa Brown backstitch

29

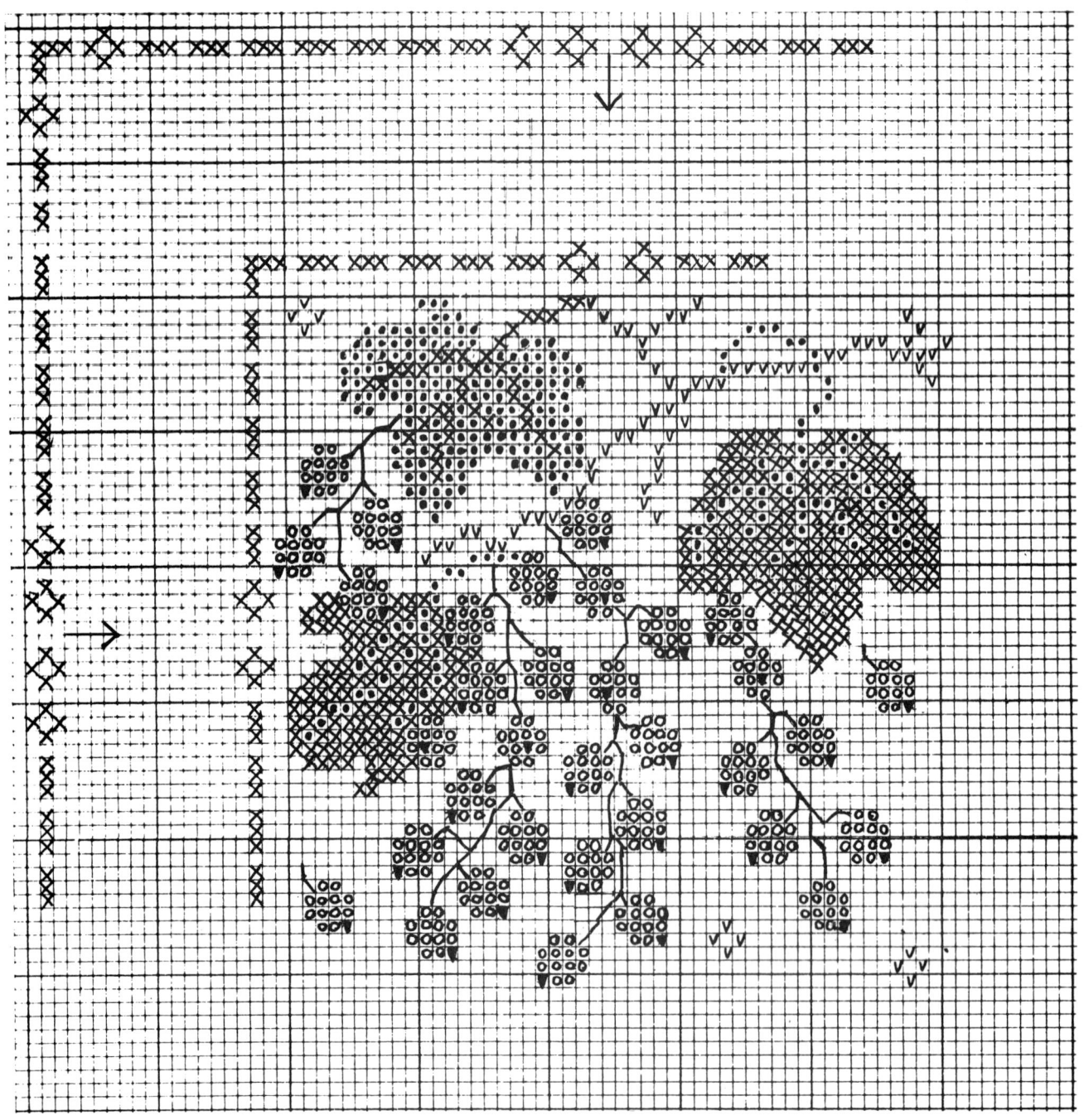

Red Currant Doily

DMC #

⊙	350	Medium Coral
▼	838	Very Dark Beige Brown
☑	433	Medium Brown
☒	905	Dark Parrot Green
⊡	906	Medium Parrot Green
—	906	Medium Parrot Green backstitch

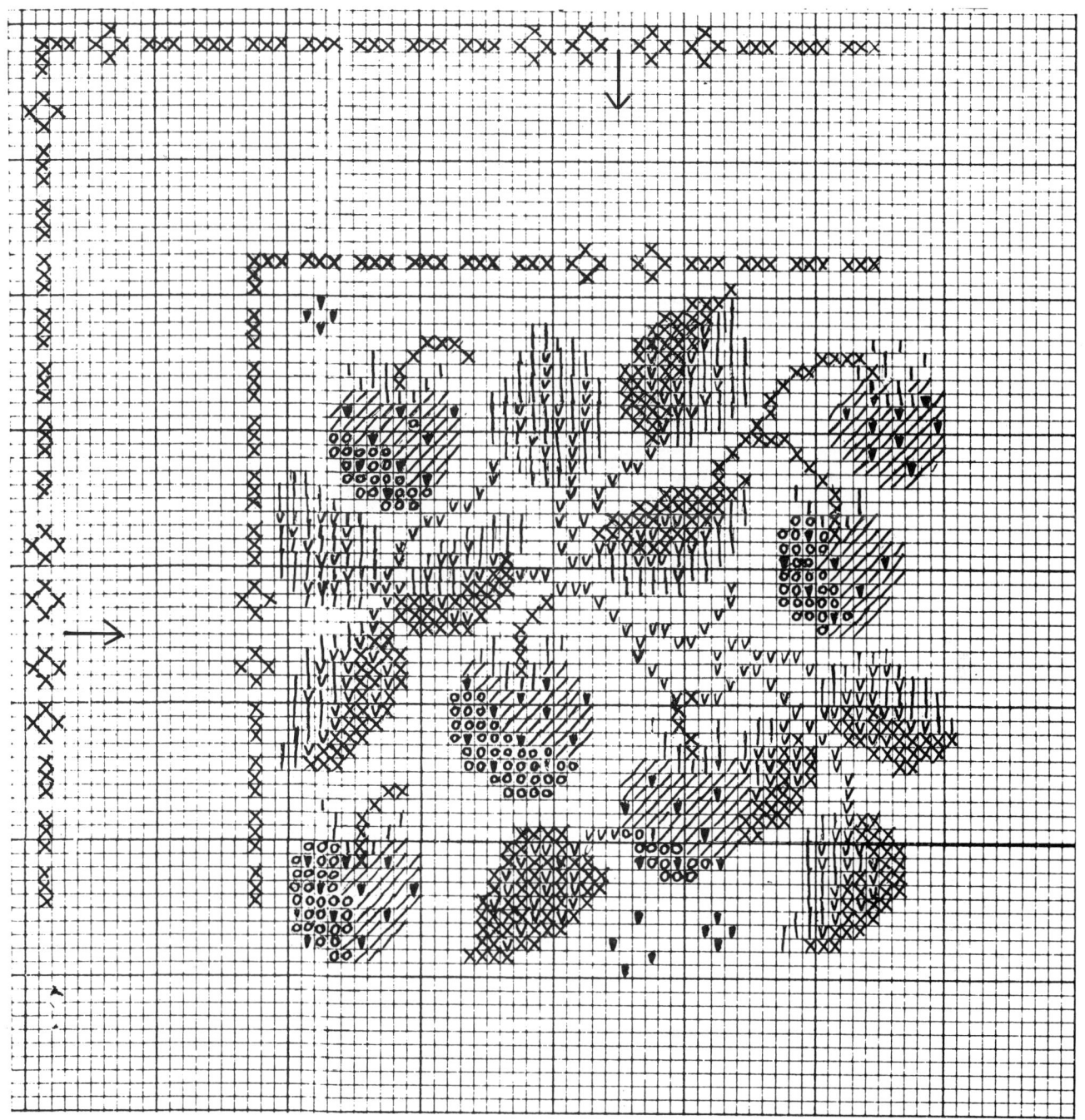

Strawberry Doily

DMC #

⊠	702	Kelly Green
⊓	703	Chartreuse
☑	3347	Medium Yellow Green
▼	734	Light Olive Green
⊙	606	Bright Orange Red
⊿	900	Dark Burnt Orange

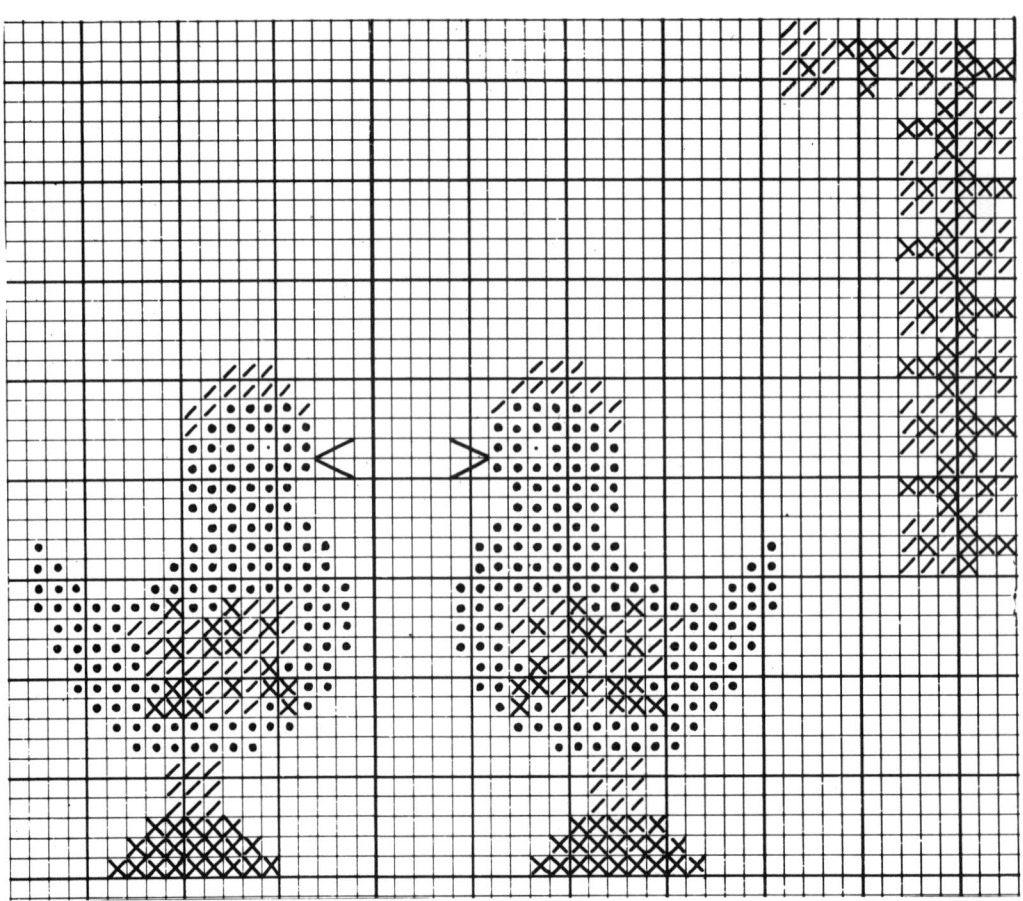

Chicks Doily ▲

DMC #

⊡	310	Black
⊘	608	Bright Orange
▬	608	Bright Orange backstitch
⊠	703	Chartreuse
⊙	726	Light Topaz

Chicks Napkin Ring ▶

DMC #

◢	310	Black
⊠	608	Bright Orange
▬	608	Bright Orange backstitch
◪	743	Dark Yellow

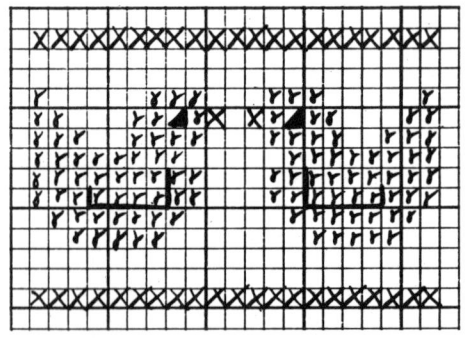

Little Chick Placemat

DMC #

■	310	Black (use 1 strand only)
☑	350	Medium Coral
—	350	Medium Coral backstitch for beak and legs
▼	701	Light Christmas Green
—	701	Light Christmas Green backstitch for border
☒	703	Chartreuse
☑	704	Bright Chartreuse
—	704	Bright Chartreuse backstitch under chick
⊞	741	Medium Tangerine
◙	725	Topaz
ℤ	972	Yellow Orange

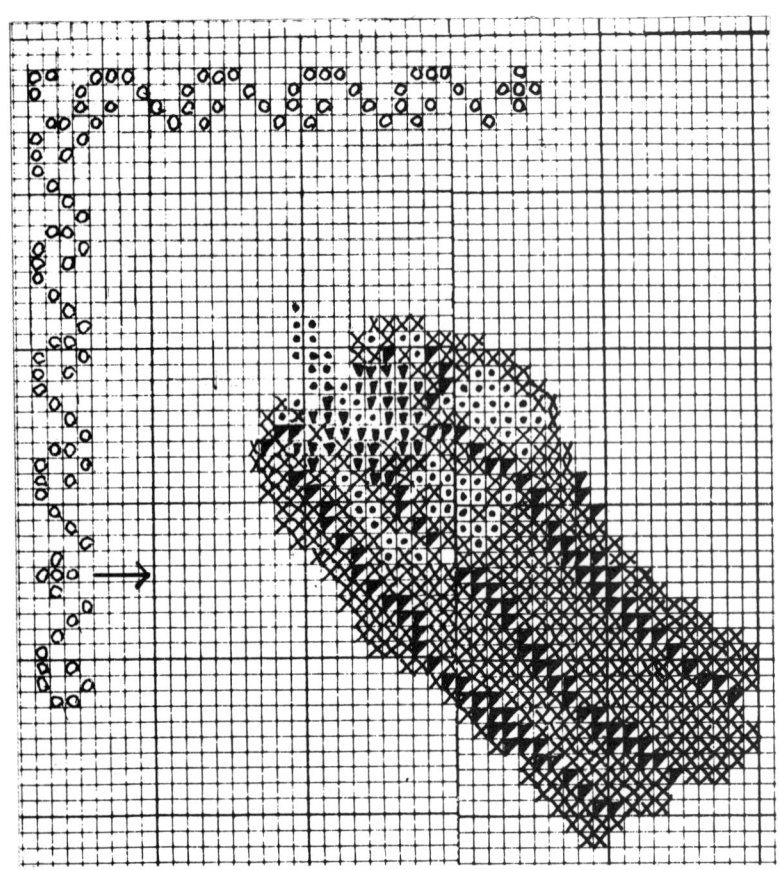

Green Pepper

DMC

⊡	349	Dark Coral
▼	699	Christmas Green
◩	700	Bright Christmas Green
☒	702	Kelly Green
⊡	704	Bright Chartreuse

Red Pepper

DMC

◢	304	Medium Christmas Red
⊡	349	Dark Coral
⊡	351	Coral
▼	699	Christmas Green
☑	701	Light Christmas Green
⊞	702	Kelly Green

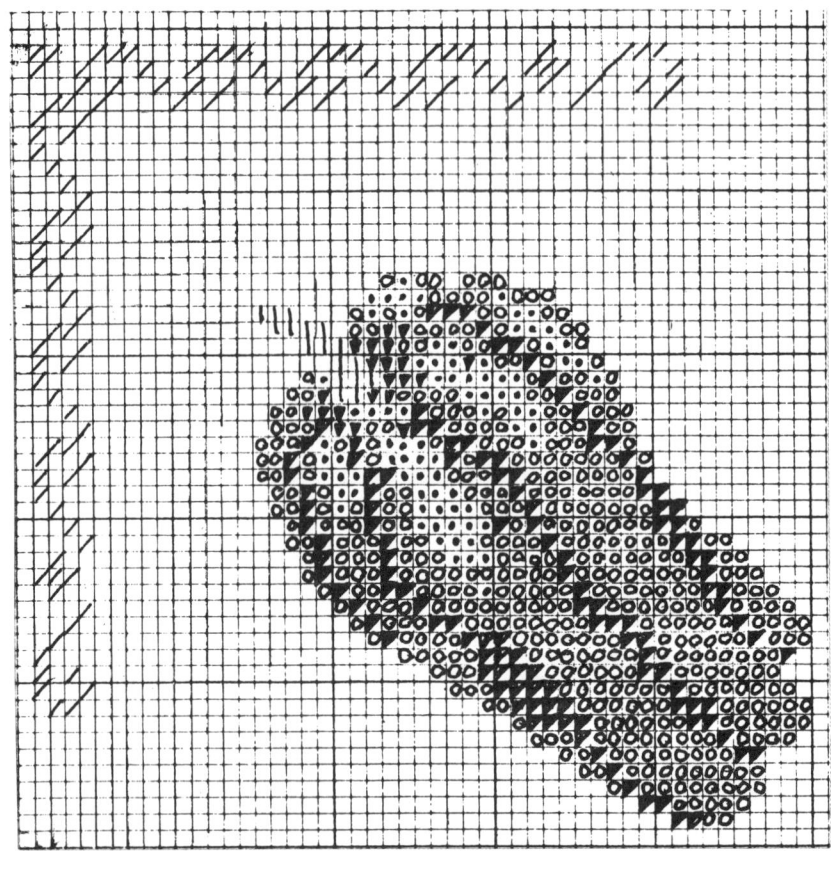

Radish Centerpiece

DMC #

◪	817	Very Dark Coral
◨	351	Coral
—	356	Medium Terra-cotta backstitch
◖	3346	Hunter Green
☒	704	Bright Chartreuse
◪	3348	Light Yellow Green
⊡		White

Radish Doily

DMC #

⊡	606	Bright Orange Red
—	610	Very Dark Drab Brown backstitch
☒	701	Light Christmas Green
◪		White

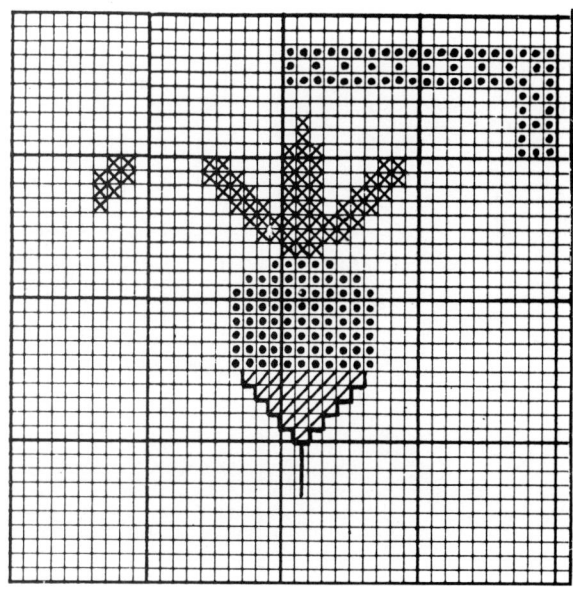

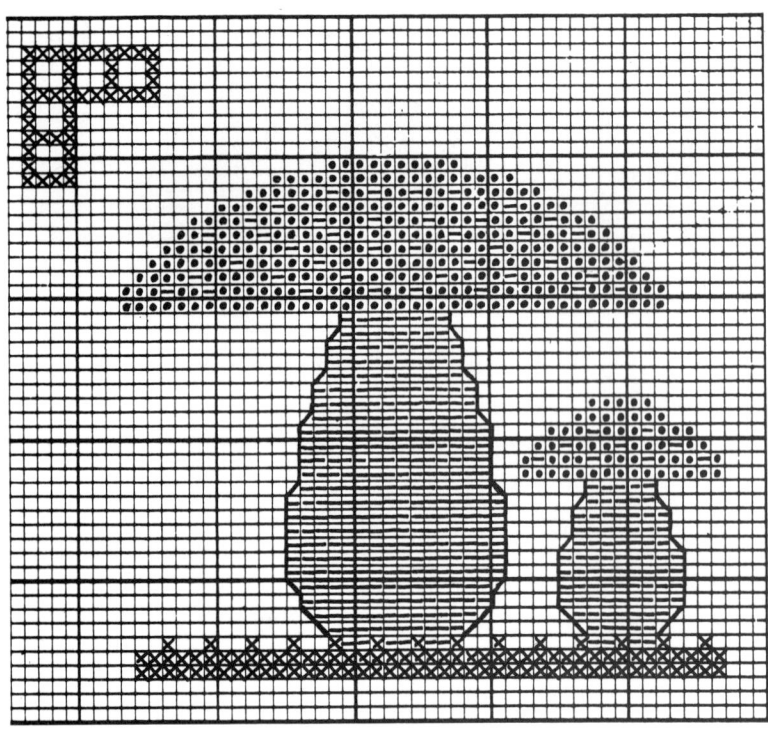

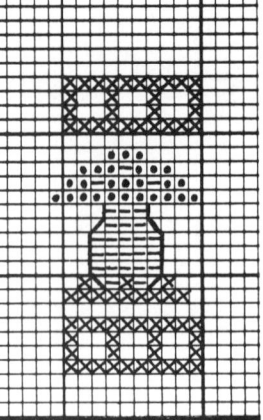

Napkin Ring

Placemat

Mushroom Luncheon Set ▲

DMC #

⊡	606	Bright Orange Red
✖	702	Kelly Green
⊟		White

Mushroom Border ▼

DMC #

⊡	666	Bright Christmas Red
✖	702	Kelly Green
⧄		White

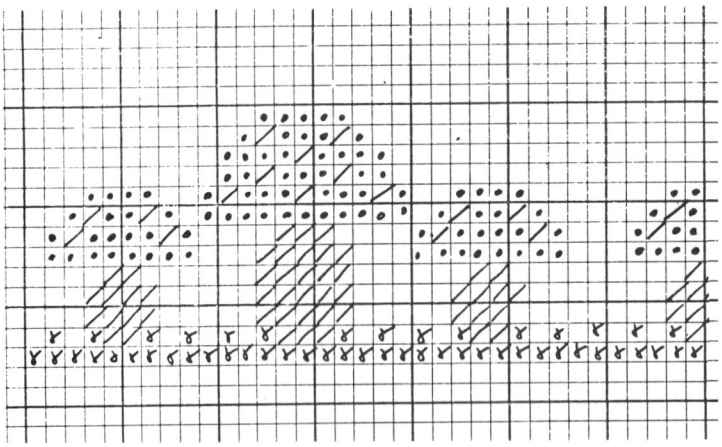

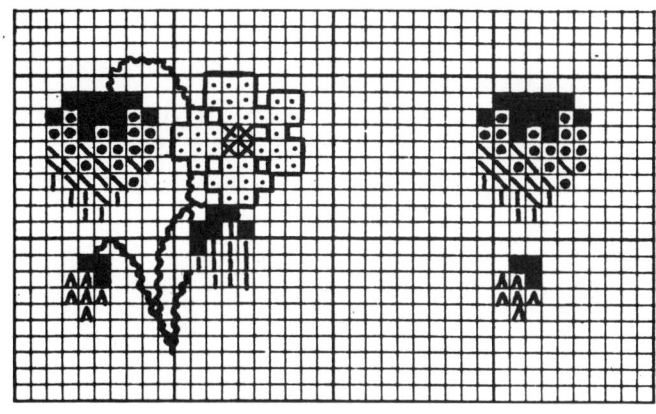

Strawberry Border

DMC

■	3346	Hunter Green
∿	581	Moss Green backstitch
⊡	3013	Light Khaki Green
—	3013	Light Khaki Green backstitch
⊙	817	Very Dark Coral
◨	350	Medium Coral
◧	352	Light Coral
⊠	444	Dark Lemon Yellow
⊡		White

Strawberry Egg Cozy ▶

DMC

☒	666	Bright Christmas Red
⧄	700	Bright Christmas Green
—	700	Bright Christmas Green back-stitch
⊍	702	Kelly Green
∣	742	Light Tangerine straight stitch

After all cross-stitches have been completed, work straight-stitch seeds with 742 Light Tangerine.

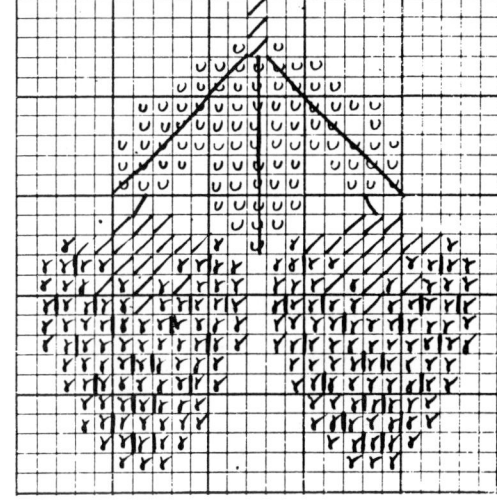

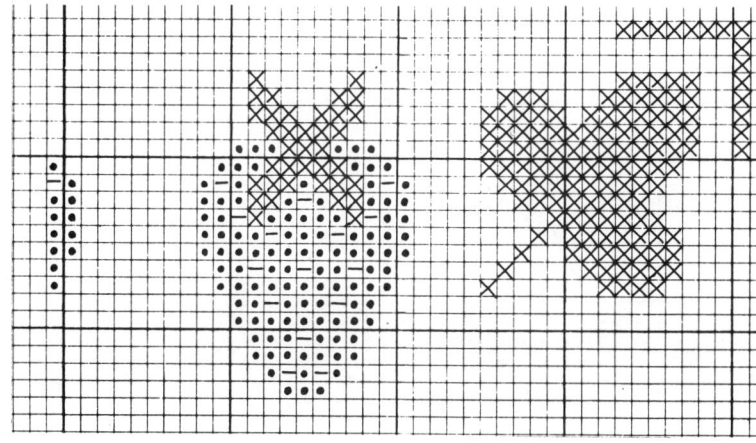

Strawberry Napkin

DMC

⊙	606	Bright Orange Red
⊠	701	Light Christmas Green
⊟		White

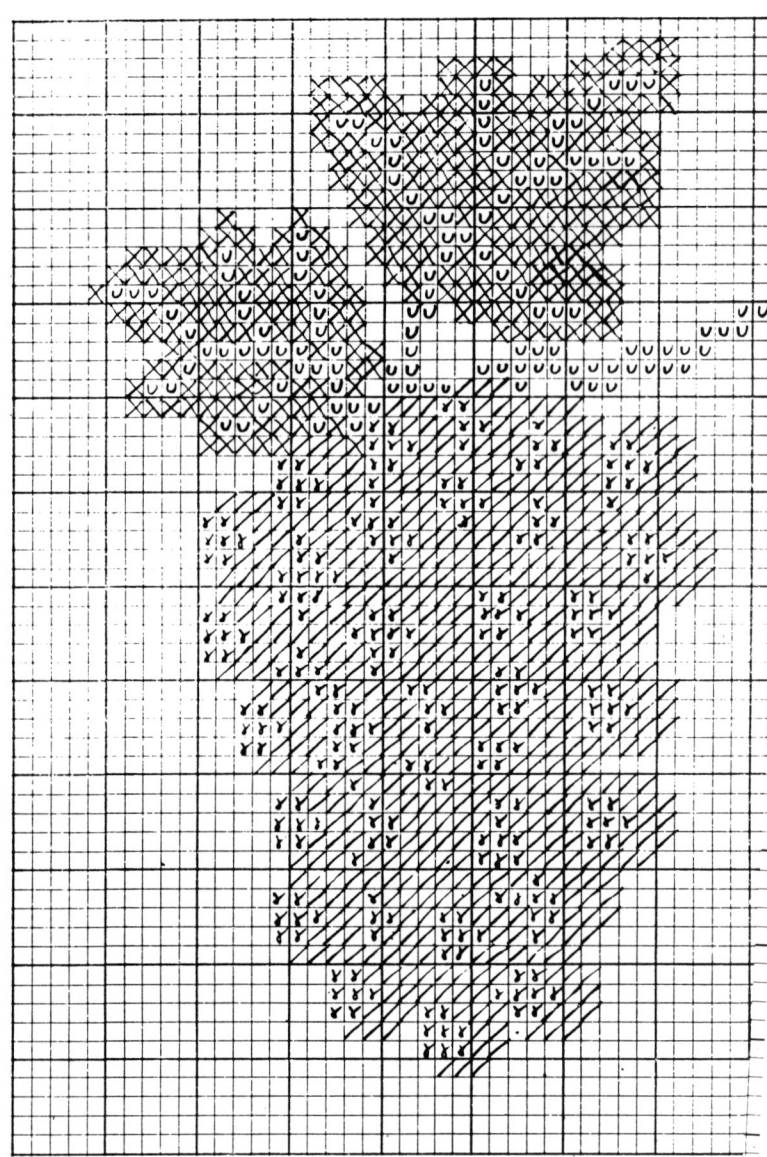

Grapes

DMC #

◱	824	Very Dark Blue
⊻	826	Medium Blue
⊠	988	Forest Green
⊍	895	Dark Christmas Green

Blueberries

DMC #

—	700	Bright Christmas Green backstitch
⊻	702	Kelly Green
⊠	824	Very Dark Blue

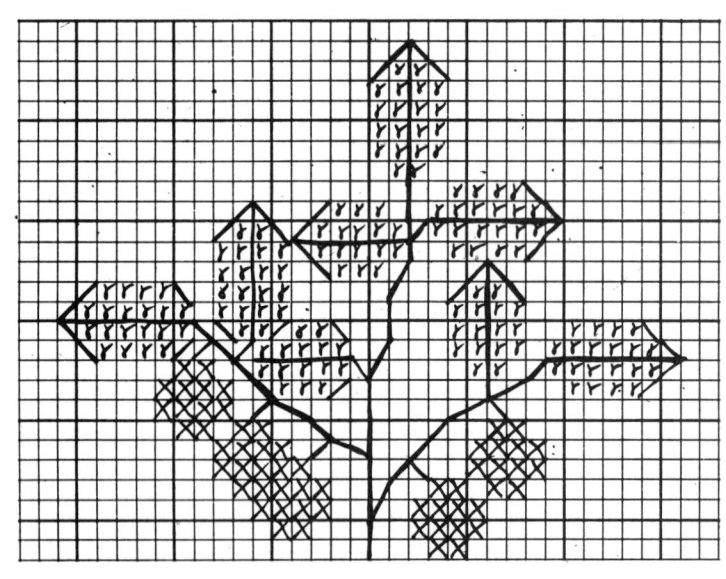

Lemon Branch

	DMC #	
—	895	Dark Christmas Green backstitch
⊡	907	Light Parrot Green
⊟	469	Avocado Green
⊍	972	Yellow Orange
ℤ	973	Bright Canary Yellow
�4	445	Light Lemon Yellow

Cherry Potholder ▶

DMC #

- ▣ 606 Bright Orange Red
- ☒ 702 Kelly Green
- — 702 Kelly Green backstitch

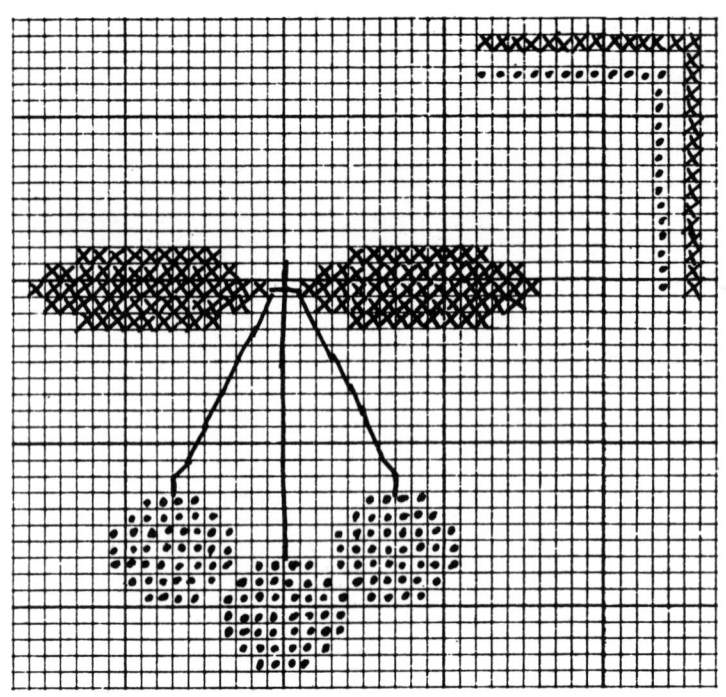

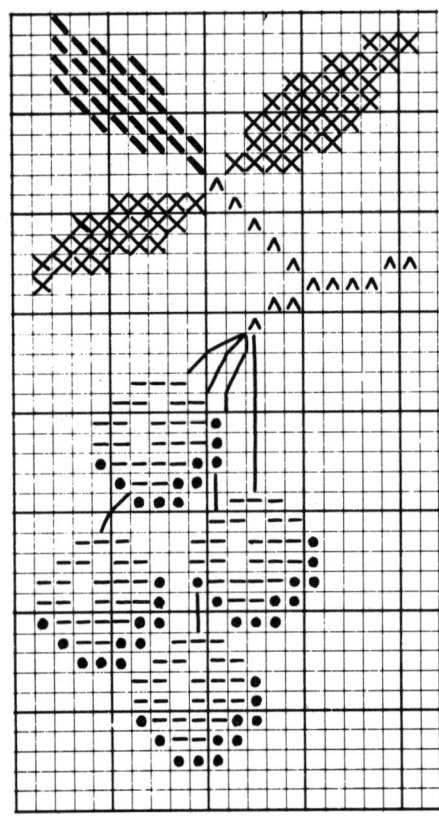

◀ Cherries Motif

DMC #

- ▣ 304 Medium Christmas Red
- ⊟ 349 Dark Coral
- ◭ 420 Dark Hazelnut Brown
- ◹ 3346 Hunter Green
- ☒ 3347 Medium Yellow Green
- — 3347 Medium Yellow Green backstitch

Cherry Doily ▶

DMC #

- ◭ 606 Bright Orange Red
- ▣ 702 Kelly Green
- — 702 Kelly Green backstitch

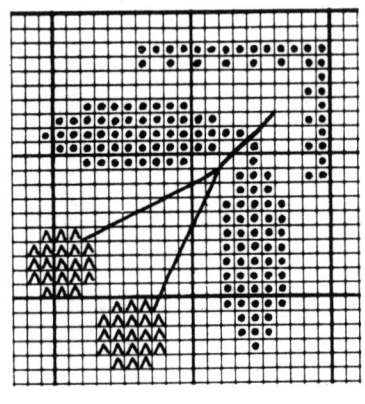

Fruit Motif Bookmark ▶

DMC #

- ⊠ 666 Bright Christmas Red
- ◩ 608 Bright Orange
- ⊿ 700 Bright Christmas Green
- ⊍ 702 Kelly Green

◄ Cherries Border

DMC #

- ◪ 301 Medium Mahogany
- ⊙ 817 Very Dark Coral
- ⊡ 350 Medium Coral
- ⊠ 3347 Medium Yellow Green
- — 3347 Medium Yellow Green backstitch
- ▽ 3348 Light Yellow Green

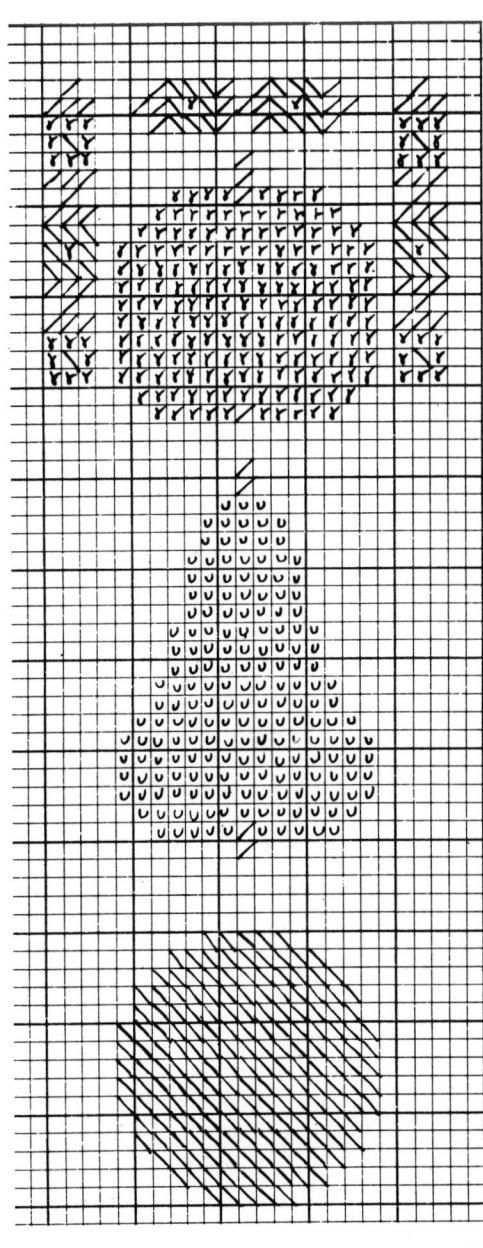

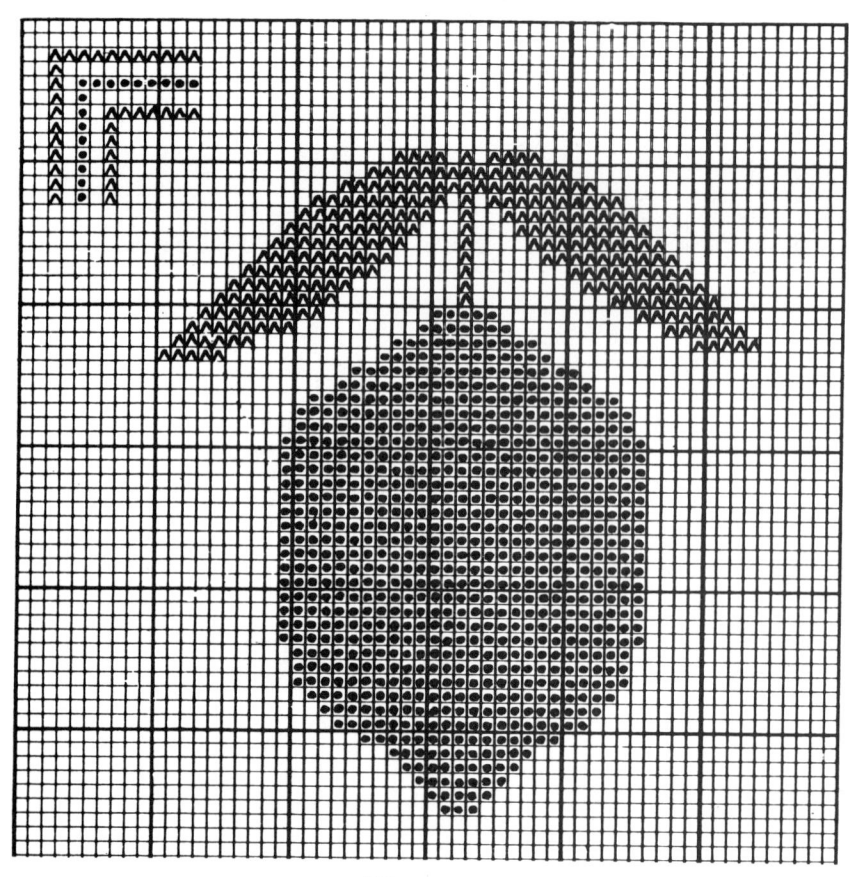

Placemat

Napkin Ring

Lemon Luncheon Set ▲

DMC
⊡ 307 Lemon Yellow
🔺 701 Light Christmas Green

Plum Luncheon Set ▼

DMC
◣ 300 Very Dark Mahogany
⧄ 700 Bright Christmas Green
⊡ 703 Chartreuse
🔺 3685 Dark Mauve

Placemat

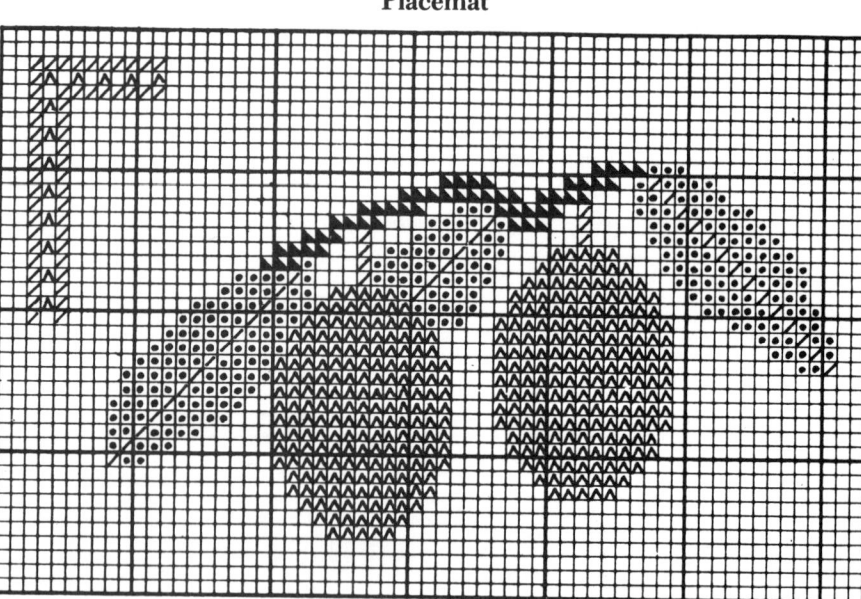

Napkin Ring

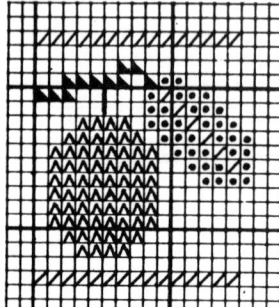

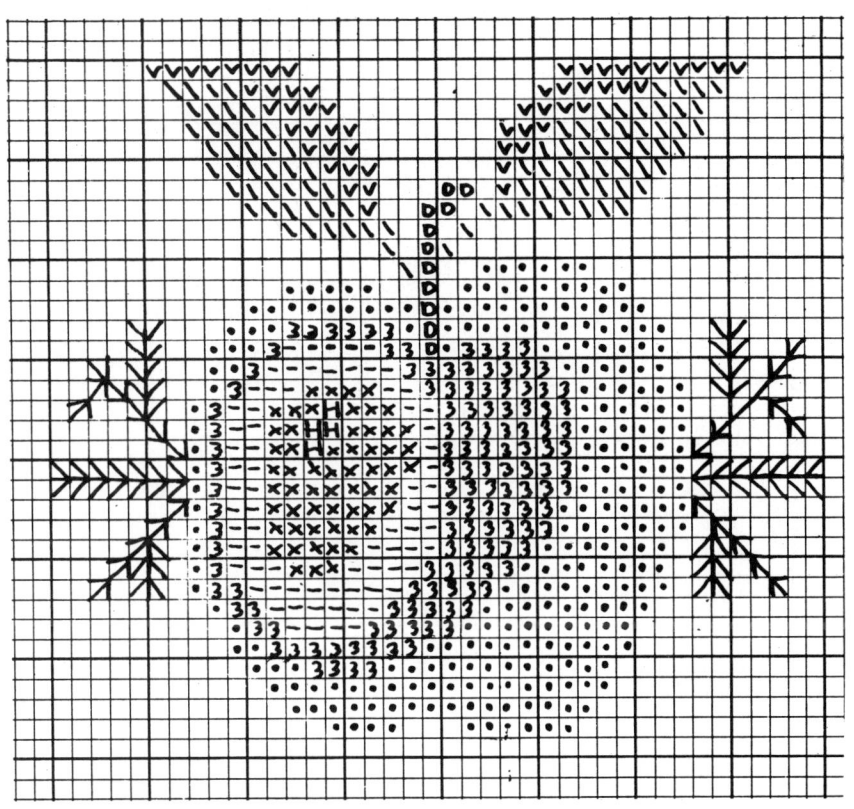

Apple Doily

DMC #

⊡	817	Very Dark Coral
3	666	Bright Christmas Red
⊟	606	Bright Orange Red
⊠	608	Bright Orange
⤸	895	Dark Christmas Green straight stitch
☑	906	Medium Parrot Green
◹	3345	Dark Hunter Green
◉	839	Dark Beige Brown
Ⓗ		White

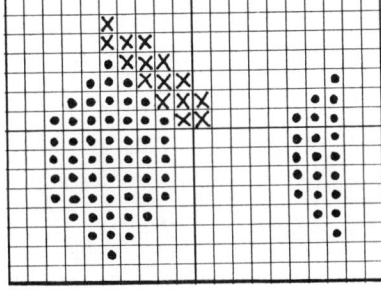

Lemon Border

DMC #

☐	310	Black (for background)
⊠	703	Chartreuse
◉	973	Bright Canary Yellow

Apple Borders

Border 1

DMC #

⊡	350	Medium Coral
⊤	352	Light Coral
⊠	433	Medium Brown
⍈	725	Topaz
⊠	470	Medium Light Avocado Green
◁	471	Light Avocado Green

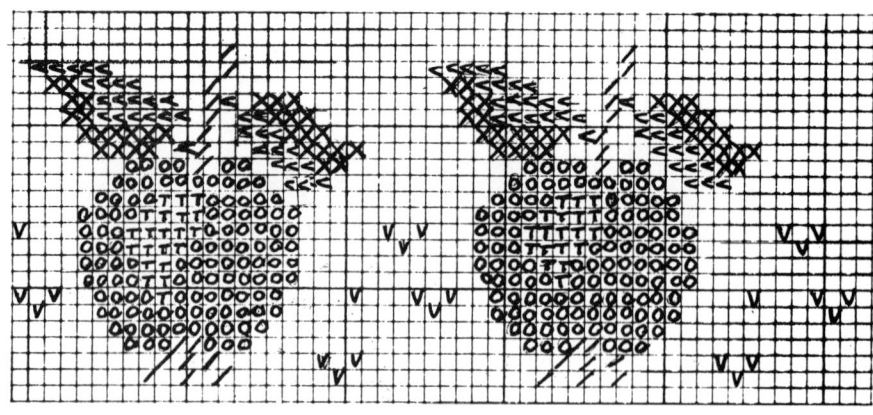

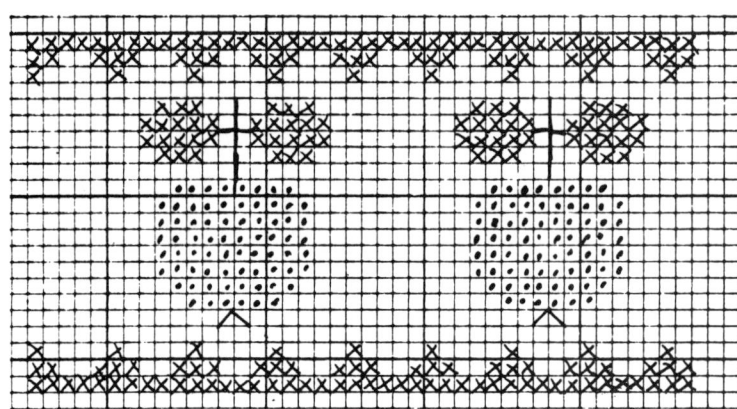

Border 2

DMC #

⊡	321	Christmas Red
⊠	3347	Medium Yellow Green
—	3347	Medium Yellow Green backstitch

Border 3

DMC #

⊘	666	Bright Christmas Red
⊙	943	Medium Aquamarine
☐	954	Nile Green (for background)
⍥	973	Bright Canary Yellow

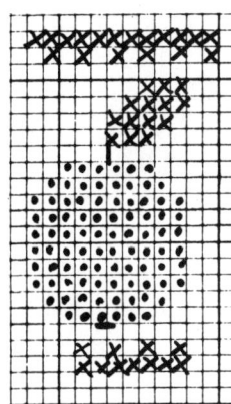

Orange Napkin Ring

DMC #

- ☒ 701   Light Christmas Green
- — 701   Light Christmas Green backstitch
- ⊡ 947   Burnt Orange

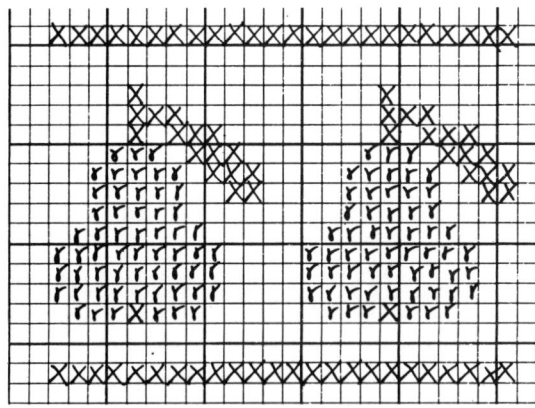

Pear Border

DMC #

- ☒ 700   Bright Christmas Green
- ⊠ 703   Chartreuse

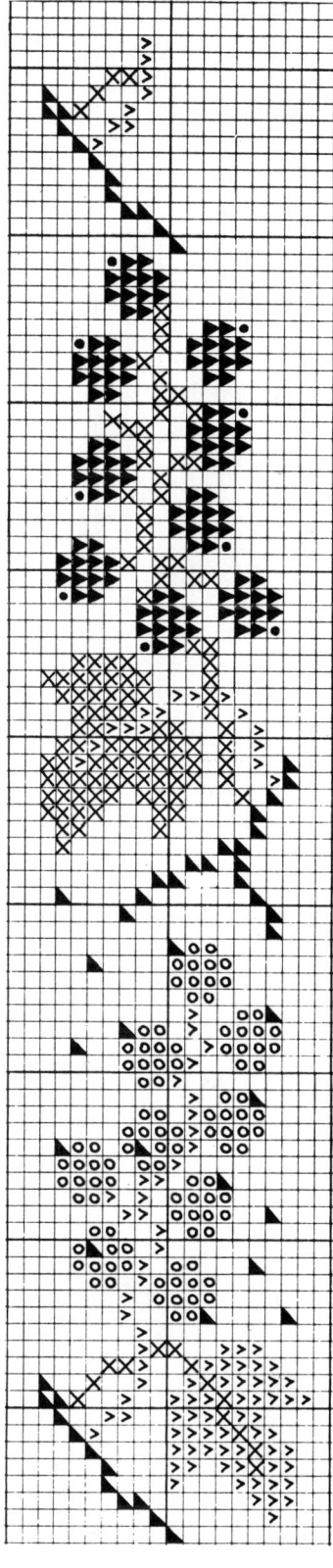

Currant Border ▶

DMC #

- ⊙ 350   Medium Coral
- ◣ 640   Very Dark Beige Gray
- ⊡ 435   Very Light Brown
- ☒ 702   Kelly Green
- ▷ 703   Chartreuse
- ▶ 939   Very Dark Navy Blue

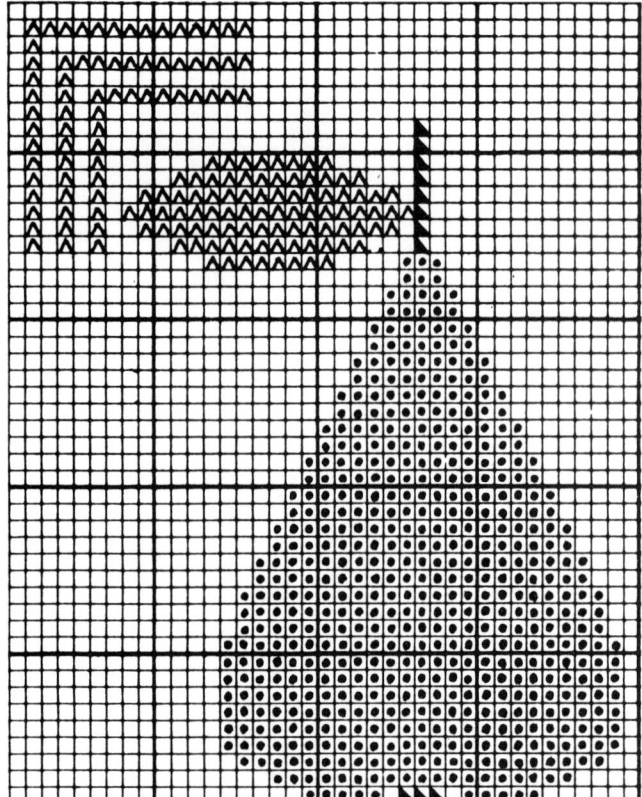

Placemat

Pear Luncheon Set

DMC #

◣ 300 Very Dark Mahogany

◣ 701 Light Christmas Green

⊡ 704 Bright Chartreuse

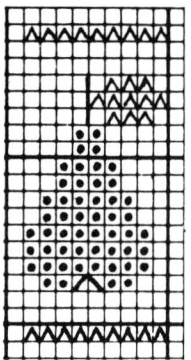

Napkin ring

Mint ▸

DMC #

⊡ 895 Dark Christmas Green

•—•— 895 Dark Christmas Green backstitch

⊠ 470 Medium Light Avocado Green

—╫—╫— 470 Medium Light Avocado Green backstitch

◩ 894 Very Light Carnation Red

〜〜〜 Metallic Gold backstitch

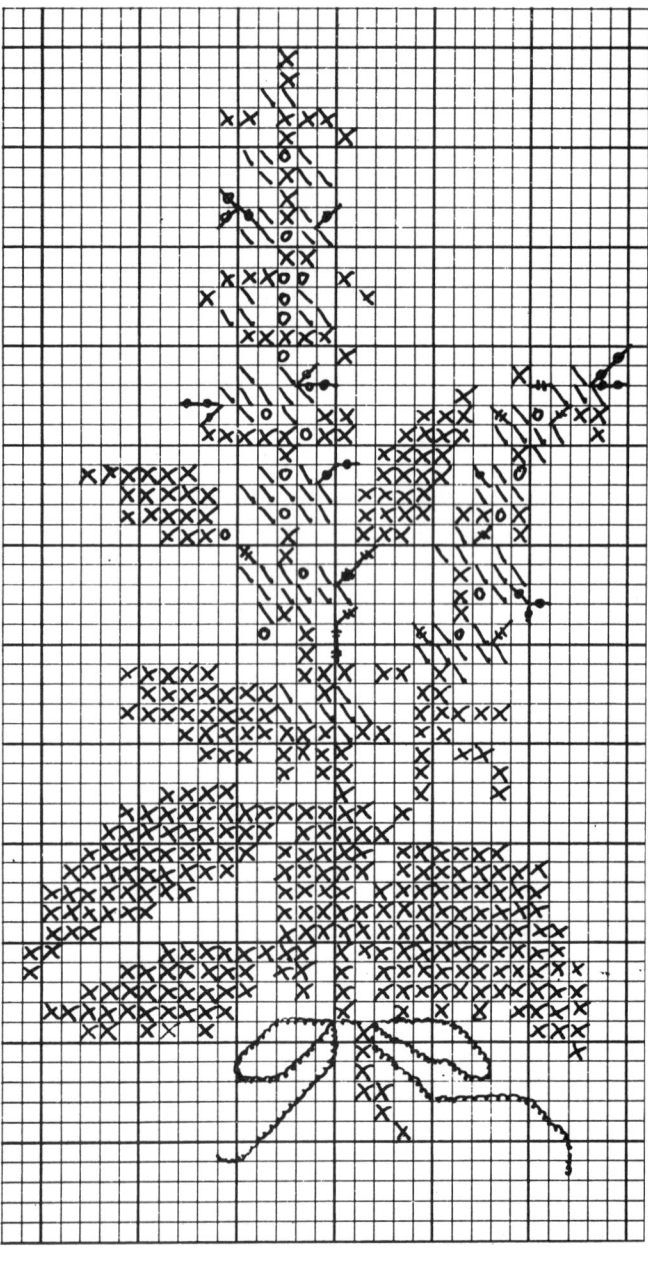

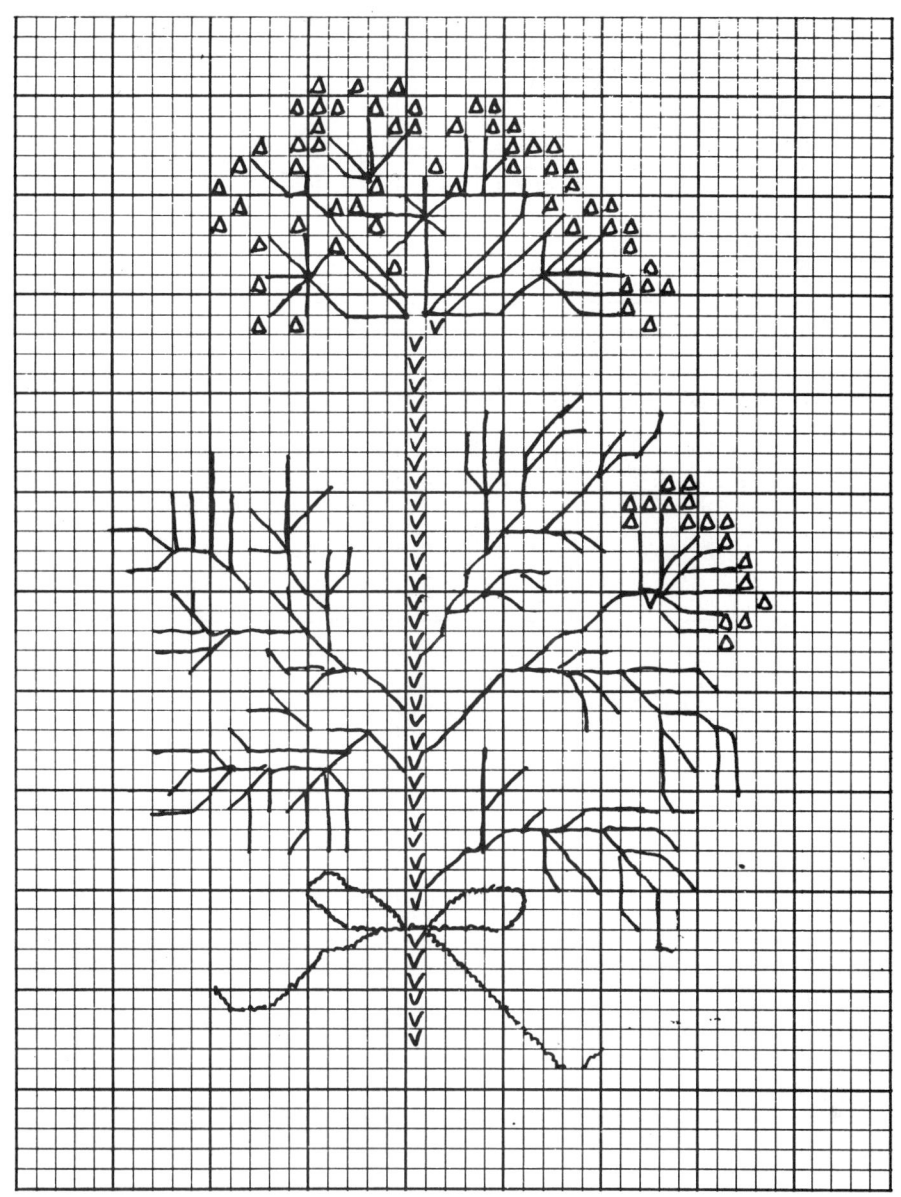

Dill

DMC #

☑	905	Dark Parrot Green
—	905	Dark Parrot Green backstitch
△	973	Bright Canary Yellow
∼∼∼		Metallic Gold backstitch

SIX STRAND EMBROIDERY COTTON (FLOSS) CONVERSION CHART

KEY: T = Possible Substitute   * = Close Match   — = No Match

DMC NO.	ROYAL MOULINÉ NO.	BATES/ANCHOR
White	1001	2
Ecru	8600	926
208	3335*	110*
209	3415*	105
210	3320*	104
211	3410	108*
221	2570	897*
223	2555	894
224	2545	893
225	2540	892
300	8330	352*
301	8315*	349*
304	2415*	47*
307	6005*	289*
309	2525*	42*
310	1002	403
311	4275T	149*
312		147*
315	3130	896*
316	3120	895*
317	1030*	400*
318	1020*	399*
319	5025	246*
320	5015	216*
321	2415	47
322		978*
326	2530*	59*
327	3365*	101*
333		119
334	4250T	145
335	2525T	42*
336	4270*	149*
340		118
341		117
347	2425*	13*
349	2400	13
350	2045T	11
351	2015T	11*
352	2015	10*
353	2010*	8*
355	8095	5968
356	8090	5975*
367	5020	216*
368	5005*	240*
369	5005	213*
370		889*
371		888*
372		887*
400	8325*	351
402	8305*	347*
407	8005	882*
413	1025*	401
414	1020*	400*
415	1015	398
420	8720*	375*
422	8710*	373*
433	8265	371*
434	8215	309
435	8210*	369*
436	8205	363*

DMC NO.	ROYAL MOULINÉ NO.	BATES/ANCHOR
437	8200*	362
444	6155*	291
445	6000	288
451		399*
452		399*
453	1015T	397*
469	5255	267*
470	5255*	267
471	5245	266*
472	5240	264*
498	2425T	20*
500	5125	879*
501	5120*	878
502	5110	876
503	5105	875
504	5100	213*
517		169*
518	4860*	168*
519	4855T	167*
520		862*
522		859*
523		859*
524	1115T	858*
535		401*
543	8500	933*
550	3380*	102*
552	3370*	101
553	3360	98
554	3355*	96*
561		212*
562		210*
563		208*
564		203*
580	5935	267*
581	5925	266*
597	4860*	168*
598	4855*	167*
600	2225*	59*
601	2225*	78*
602	2640*	77*
603	2720*	76*
604	2710	75*
605	2155	50*
606	7260	335
608	7255	333*
610	5825T	889*
611	5735T	898
612	8815*	832
613	5605*	956*
632	8530	936*
640	8625	903
642	8620*	392
644	8800	830
645	1115	905*
646	1115*	8581*
647	1110	8581*
648	1100*	900
666	2405	46
676	6250	891
677		886*

DMC NO.	ROYAL MOULINÉ NO.	BATES/ANCHOR
680	6260*	901
699	5375	923*
700	5365*	229
701	5365*	227
702	5330	239
703	5320	238
704	5310*	256*
712	8600*	387*
718	3015*	88
720		326
721		324*
722		323*
725	6215	306*
726	6150*	295
727	6135	293
729	6255	890
730		924*
731	5925T	281*
732		281*
733		280*
734		279*
738	8245*	942
739	8240*	885*
740	7045	316
741	6125	304
742	6120	303
743	6210	297
744	6110*	301*
745	6105	300*
746	6100	386*
747	4850	158*
754	8075	778*
758	8080	868
760	2035	9*
761	2030	8*
762	1010*	397
772	4600*	264*
775	2110*	128*
776	3110	24*
778		968*
780	8215*	310*
781	8215	309*
782	6230	308
783	6220*	307
791	4165*	941*
792	4155T	940
793	4155	121
794	4145	120*
796	4340	133*
797	4265*	132*
798	4325	131*
799	4250*	130*
800	4310	128
801	8405	357*
806	4870T	169*
807	4860*	168*
809	4145*	130*
813	4610*	160*
814	2340T	44*
815	2530*	43

DMC NO.	ROYAL MOULINÉ NO.	BATES/ANCHOR
816	2530	44*
817	2415T	19
818	2505*	48
819	2000	892*
820	4345	134
822	8605*	387*
823	4400*	150
824	4225	164*
825	4215	162*
826	4210	161*
827	4605	159*
828	4850	158*
829	5825	906
830	5825*	889*
831	5825T	889*
832	5815	907
833	5815*	874*
834	5810*	874
838	8425*	380
839	8560	380*
840	8555	379*
841	8550	378*
842	8505	376*
844	1115T	401*
869	8720*	944*
890	5025*	879*
891	2135	35*
892	2130	28
893	2125*	27
894	2115T	26
895	5430*	246*
898	8425*	360
899	2515	27*
902	7230*	333
904	5295*	258*
905	5295	258*
906	5285*	256*
907	5280*	255
909	5370	229*
910	5370*	228*
911	5465*	205*
912	5465	205
913	5460*	209
915	3030	89*
917	3020*	89*
918	8330*	341*
919	8095*	341*
920	8060*	339*
921	8060T	349*
922	8315T	324*
924	4830T	851*
926	4820*	779*
927	4810T	849*
928	1010T	900*
930	4510	922*
931	4505	921*
932	4500	920*
934	5070T	862*
935	5225T	862*

DMC NO.	ROYAL MOULINÉ NO.	BATES/ANCHOR
936	5260T	269
937	5260	268
938	8430	381
939	4405	127
943	4935*	188*
945	8020*	347*
946	7230*	332*
947	7255*	330*
948	8070	778*
950	8020T	4146
951	8020T	366*
954	5455*	203*
955	5450	206*
956	2170*	40*
957	2160T	40*
958		187
959		186
961	2515*	76*
962	2515	76*
963	2505	49*
964		185
966	5150*	214*
970	7040	316*
971	7045	316*
972	6120*	298
973	6015	290
975	8365	355*
976	8355	308*
977	8350	307*
986	5430	246*
987	5020T	244*
988	5295T	243*
989	5405T	242*
991	5165T	189*
992	4925*	187*
993	4915*	186*
995	4710	410
996	4700	433
3011	5525T	845*
3012	5525*	844*
3013	5515	842*
3021	5430*	382*
3022		8581*
3023		8581*
3024	1100	900*
3031		905*
3032	8620T	903*
3033	8610*	388*
3041	3215*	871
3042	3205*	869
3045	6260T	373*
3046	5810	887*
3047	5805	886*
3051	5530T	846*
3052	5060*	859*
3053	5055*	859*
3064	8005*	914*
3072	4805*	397*
3078	6130	292*
3325	4200	159*

DMC NO.	ROYAL MOULINÉ NO.	BATES/ANCHOR
3326	2115*	25*
3328	2045	11*
3340		329
3341		328
3345	5025T	268*
3346	5220T	257*
3347	5210*	266*
3348	5270*	265
3350	2220	42*
3354	2210	74*
3362		862*
3363		861*
3364		843*
3371	8435	382
3607		87*
3608		86
3609		85
3685	2335	70*
3687	2325	69*
3688	2320	66*
3689	2310	49
3705		35*
3706		28*
3708		26*
48	9000*	1201*
51	9014	1220
52	9006	1208
53		—
57	9002	1203
61	9013T	1218*
62	9000T	1201*
67		1211*
69		1218*
75	9002	1206*
90	9012T	1217*
91	9008*	1211
92	9012	1216*
93	9007*	1210*
94	9011*	1216
95	9006T	1208*
99	9005T	1207*
101	9009*	1213*
102		1208*
103		1210*
104	9012	1217
105	9013*	1228
106	9002T	1203*
107	9003	1204
108	9014*	1220*
111		1218*
112	9003T	1204*
113	9007*	1210*
114	9010	1215
115	9004	1206
121	9007	1210
122	9010T	1215*
123		1213*
124	9007T	1210*
125	9009	1213
126	9006*	1208*